# REVISE AQA GCSE
# Science A
# Additional Science
# REVISION GUIDE
# Foundation

Authors: Sue Kearsey, Nigel Saunders and Peter Ellis

## THE REVISE AQA SERIES

Available in online

Other titles in the Revise AQA series are available

On the eLearn platform, you can view the full book and add notes, comments and weblinks.

| | |
|---|---|
| Revision Guide Foundation | 9781447942177 |
| Revision Workbook Foundation | 9781447942481 |
| Revision Guide Foundation | 9781447942115 |
| Revision Workbook Foundation | 9781447942252 |

Titles are also available for Science (Foundation and Higher), Additional Science (Higher) and Further Additional.

This book is designed to complement your classroom and home study to help prepare you for the exam. It does not include all the content and skills needed for the complete course. It is designed to work in combination with Pearson's main AQA GCSE Science 2011 Series.

**To find out more visit:**
www.pearsonschools.co.uk/aqagcsesciencerevision

ALWAYS LEARNING                    PEARSON

# Contents

**1-to-1** page match with the Additional Foundation Workbook ISBN 978-1-447-94248-1

## BIOLOGY
1. Animal and plant cells
2. Different kinds of cells
3. Diffusion
4. Organisation of the body
5. Organs and organ systems
6. Plant organs
7. Photosynthesis
8. Limiting factors
9. **Biology six mark question 1**
10. Distribution of organisms
11. Sampling organisms
12. Transect sampling
13. Proteins
14. Digestive enzymes
15. Microbial enzymes
16. Aerobic respiration
17. The effect of exercise
18. Anaerobic respiration
19. **Biology six mark question 2**
20. Mitosis
21. Sexual reproduction
22. Stem cells
23. Genes and alleles
24. Genetic diagrams
25. Mendel's work
26. Punnett squares
27. Family trees
28. Embryo screening
29. Fossils
30. Extinction
31. **Biology six mark question 3**

## CHEMISTRY
32. Forming ions
33. Ionic compounds
34. Giant ionic structures
35. Covalent bonds in simple molecules
36. Covalent bonds in macromolecules
37. Properties of molecules
38. Properties of ionic compounds
39. Metals
40. Polymers
41. Nanoscience
42. Different structures
43. **Chemistry six mark question 1**
44. Atomic structure and isotopes
45. Relative formula mass
46. Paper chromatography
47. Gas chromatography
48. Percentage composition
49. Reaction yields
50. Reversible reactions
51. Rates of reaction
52. Changing rates 1
53. Changing rates 2
54. **Chemistry six mark question 2**
55. Energy changes
56. Acids and alkalis
57. Making salts
58. Making soluble salts
59. Making insoluble salts
60. Using electricity
61. Useful substances from electrolysis
62. Electrolysis products
63. **Chemistry six mark question 3**

## PHYSICS
64. Resultant forces
65. Forces and motion
66. Distance–time graphs
67. Acceleration and velocity
68. Forces and braking
69. Falling objects
70. Forces and terminal velocity
71. Elasticity
72. Forces and energy
73. KE and GPE
74. Momentum
75. **Physics six mark question 1**
76. Static electricity
77. Current and potential difference
78. Circuit diagrams
79. Resistors
80. Series and parallel
81. Variable resistance
82. Using electrical circuits
83. Different currents
84. Three-pin plugs
85. Electrical safety
86. Current and power
87. **Physics six mark question 2**
88. Atomic structure
89. Background radiation
90. Alpha, beta and gamma radiation
91. Half-life
92. Uses and dangers
93. The nuclear model of the atom
94. Nuclear fission
95. Nuclear fusion
96. The lifecycle of stars
97. **Physics six mark question 3**
98. Periodic Table
99. Chemistry Data Sheet
100. Physics Equation Sheet
101. Skills stickers
103. ISA support pages

107. Answers
114. Six mark question answers
118. Imprint

---

### A small bit of small print

AQA publishes Sample Assessment Material and the Specification on its website. This is the official content and this book should be used in conjunction with it. The questions in *Now try this* have been written to help you practise every topic in the book. Remember: the real exam questions may not look like this.

### Target grades

Target grade ranges are quoted in this book for some of the questions. Students targeting this grade range should be aiming to get most of the marks available. Students targeting a higher grade should be aiming to get all of the marks available.

Had a look ☐   Nearly there ☐   Nailed it! ☐    **BIOLOGY 2.1.1**

# Animal and plant cells

Humans and other animals are made of cells. Plants and algae are also made of cells. Most of these cells have the following parts.

**GENERALISED ANIMAL CELL**

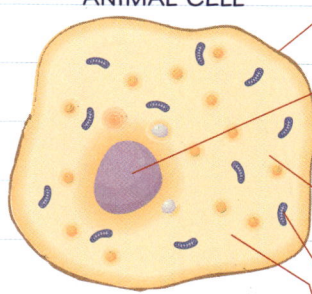

**CELL MEMBRANE:** controls what enters and leaves the cell, e.g. oxygen, carbon dioxide, glucose

**NUCLEUS:** a large structure that contains genes that control the activities of the cell

**CYTOPLASM:** jelly-like substance that fills the cell – many reactions take place here

**MITOCHONDRIA** (single: mitochondrion): tiny structures where respiration takes place, releasing energy for cell processes

**RIBOSOMES** (present in the cytoplasm but not visible at this size): where proteins are made (protein synthesis)

**GENERALISED PLANT OR ALGAL CELL**
- cell wall
- central vacuole
- chloroplasts

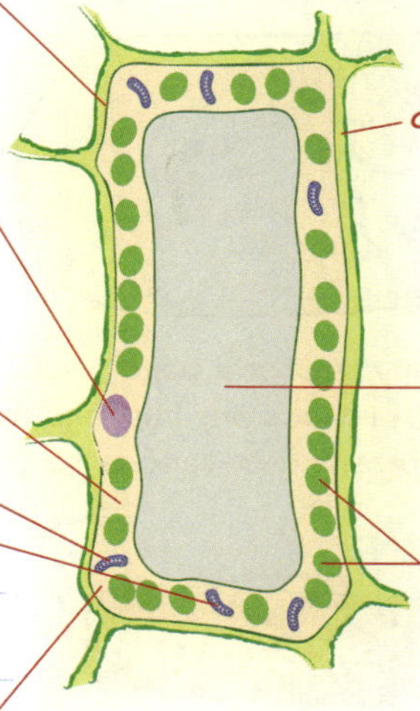

> The cytoplasm of a cell is not a structure like a chloroplast or ribosome. It is the jelly-like substance that fills a cell and supports other structures.

> Remember that every cell has a cell membrane but not all cells have a cell wall. Animal cells never have a cell wall.

## Worked example  (target D-C)

Identify **three** structures from the list below that are found in most plant and algal cells but not in animal cells, and describe their functions.
(3 marks)

nucleus, cell membrane, cell wall, cytoplasm, vacuole, chloroplast, mitochondria

Chloroplasts are the structures that absorb light energy to make food for the plant cell.
The cell wall is made of cellulose, and is strong so that it helps support the cell and helps it keep its shape.
The large permanent vacuole contains cell sap, which helps to keep the plant cell rigid.

## Now try this

**target G-E**

1. Complete the table about some parts of plant and animal cells. (4 marks)

| Cell part | Found in plant cells? | Found in animal cells? | Function |
|---|---|---|---|
| cell membrane | yes | | controls the movement of substances into and out of the cell |
| cell wall | | no | gives cell a strong shape |
| mitochondria | yes | yes | |
| nucleus | yes | yes | |

**target D-C**

2. Explain why plant and algal cells contain chloroplasts but animal cells do not. (2 marks)

1

# BIOLOGY 2.1.1

Had a look ☐   Nearly there ☐   Nailed it! ☐

# Different kinds of cells

Bacterial cells have a simpler cell structure than plant and animal cells.

- The GENES form a loop that is not in a nucleus.
- cell membrane
- Many bacteria have a CELL WALL for protection, but it is made of different substances to plant cell walls.

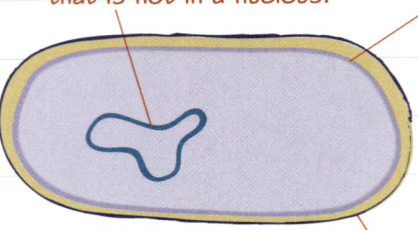

YEAST is a single-celled fungus. Yeast cells have some structures that are similar to those seen in plant and animal cells. Cell walls in plants and yeast cells are made of different materials.

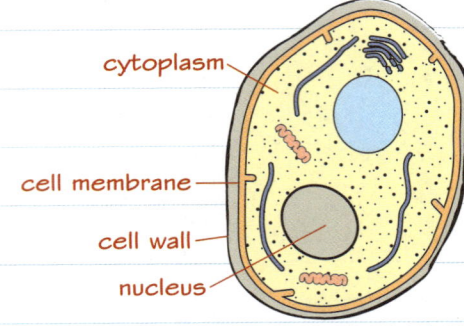

- cytoplasm
- cell membrane
- cell wall
- nucleus

## Worked example (target G-E)

Many cells are specialised to carry out a particular function. The diagrams show three specialised human cells. Draw **one** line from each cell to the box that describes the function of that cell. *(3 marks)*

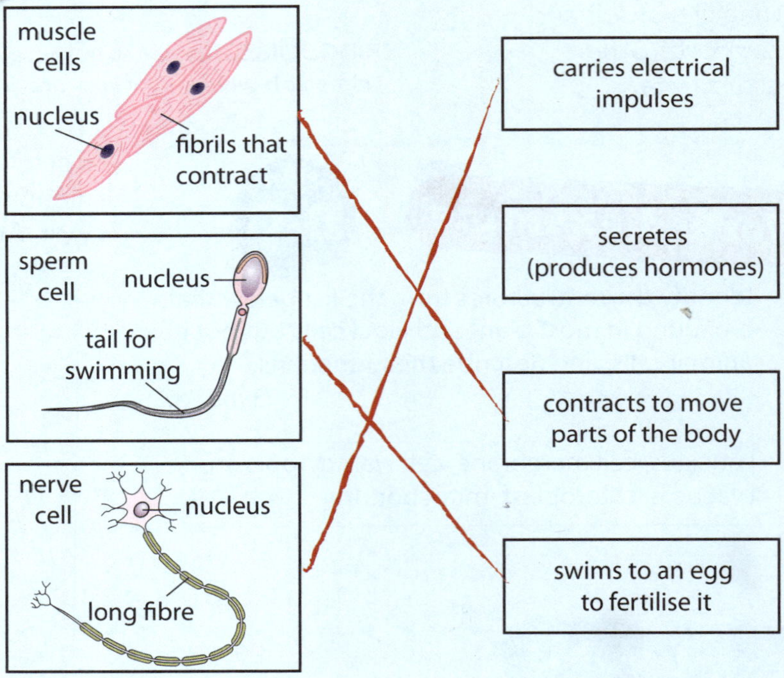

- muscle cells — nucleus — fibrils that contract → contracts to move parts of the body
- sperm cell — nucleus — tail for swimming → swims to an egg to fertilise it
- nerve cell — nucleus — long fibre → carries electrical impulses

Other boxes:
- carries electrical impulses
- secretes (produces hormones)
- contracts to move parts of the body
- swims to an egg to fertilise it

*Anything with this Spec Skills sticker is helping you to apply your knowledge.*

(AQA SKILL: Draw, Page 101)
(AQA SKILL: Evaluate, Page 101)

## Now try this

**target G-E**
1. (a) In a bacterial cell where would you find the genes? *(1 mark)*
   (b) Where would you find the genes in a human cell? *(1 mark)*

**target D-C**
2. Describe **two** ways in which a yeast cell differs from a plant cell. *(2 marks)*
3. Explain why a leaf cell contains chloroplasts. *(2 marks)*

## EXAM ALERT!

Make sure that you can recognise an unusual feature of a cell, which may be a specialisation for the function the cell carries out.

Students have struggled with questions like this in recent exams – **be prepared!**

Had a look ☐  Nearly there ☐  Nailed it! ☐   **BIOLOGY 2.1.2**

# Diffusion

Diffusion is the spreading out of particles in a gas, or of the particles of a substance in a solution.

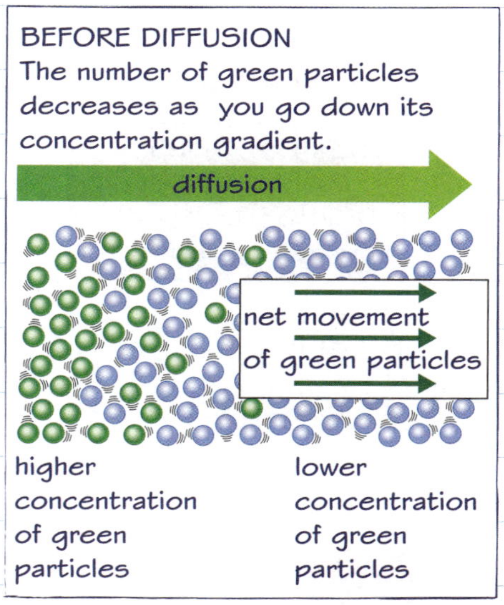

**BEFORE DIFFUSION**
The number of green particles decreases as you go down its concentration gradient.

higher concentration of green particles — lower concentration of green particles

Particles are always moving. Where there is a concentration gradient:
- more particles will be moving from the area of higher concentration
- fewer particles will be moving from the area of lower concentration.

**NET MOVEMENT** is the sum of movement of all the particles. In diffusion, the net movement is from the area of high concentration to an area of lower concentration.

**AFTER DIFFUSION**
There is no concentration gradient – the particles are evenly mixed. (The particles are still moving around though.)

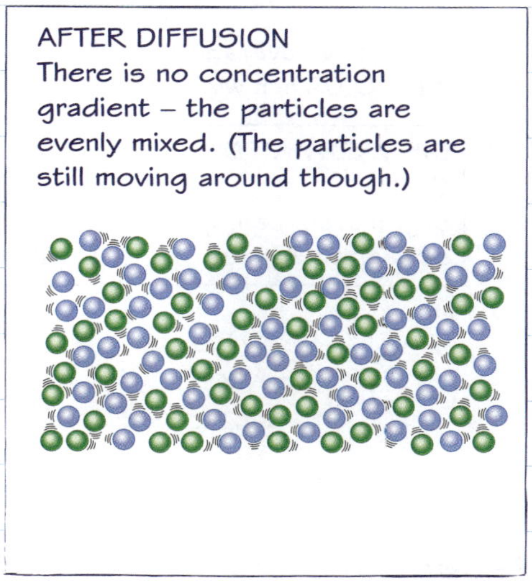

Many dissolved substances (such as glucose and mineral salts) and gases (such as oxygen and carbon dioxide) can cross cell membranes by diffusion.

The greater the difference in concentration between the two regions, the faster the rate of diffusion.

## Worked example (target G-E)

Use words from the word box to complete the sentences about movement of oxygen into cells. *(3 marks)*

| cell membrane   concentration |
| cytoplasm   diffusion   osmosis |

During respiration cells use oxygen and its _concentration_ falls inside the cell. Oxygen passes through the _cell membrane_ into the cell by a process called _diffusion_.

### EXAM ALERT!

When describing diffusion, make sure you can state what is meant by net movement from high to low concentration.

Students have struggled with exam questions similar to this – **be prepared!**

## Now try this

**(target G-E)**
1. The diagram shows cells in two solutions. In which diagram will the particles be diffusing out of the cell? *(1 mark)*

**(target D-C)**
2. Write down the meaning of: **(a)** net movement, and **(b)** diffusion. *(2 marks)*

3. Explain your answer to Question 1. *(2 marks)*

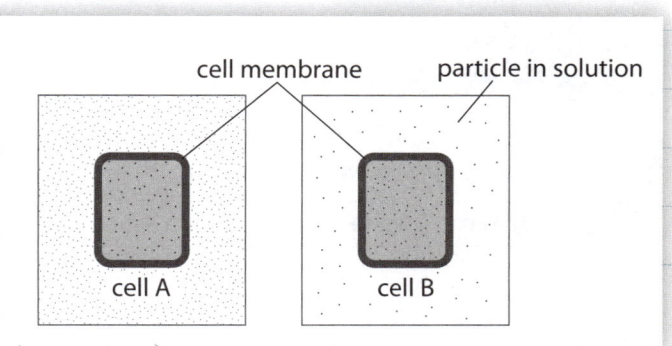

cell membrane    particle in solution

cell A    cell B

# BIOLOGY 2.1.2

Had a look ☐   Nearly there ☐   Nailed it! ☐

# Organisation of the body

Large multicellular organisms, such as humans, have bodies that are organised into different organ systems.

smallest (an average human cell is 0.05 mm wide) → increasing size → largest

| DIFFERENTIATED CELLS e.g. muscle cell, gland cell, epithelial cell | TISSUES e.g. muscular tissue, glandular tissue, epithelial tissue | ORGANS e.g. heart, stomach, skin | ORGAN SYSTEMS e.g. digestive system, circulatory system, hormonal system |

Many organ systems, such as the digestive system, exchange substances between the body and the environment.

## Tissues

During development, cells specialise to perform different functions. A tissue is a group of specialised cells that have a similar structure and function.

- **Nerve tissue** carries electrical signals around the body and in the brain. Made of nerve cells that often have long fibres to carry the electric signals.
- **Epithelial tissue** covers the surface (as skin) and lines all tubes. Made from epithelial cells that make a continuous surface.
- **Skeletal tissue** supports and protects the body. Includes bone cells that form hard bone.
- **Muscle tissue** helps the body to move. Made of muscle cells that can contract.

### Worked example   target D-C

Where is glandular tissue found, and what does it do?   *(2 marks)*

Glandular tissue is found in glands, such as the pancreas and salivary glands. Glandular cells in glandular tissue secrete substances, such as hormones or enzymes.

When you study a new organ system of the body, remember to think about the organs, tissues and differentiated cells that it is made of.

## Now try this

**1** *(target G-E)* Put the following structures in order of size, starting with the largest:

organ   tissue   cell   organ system

*(1 mark)*

**2** *(target G-E)* Give **two** examples of tissues in the human body.   *(2 marks)*

**3** *(target D-C)* Give the meaning of the term **tissue**.   *(1 mark)*

Had a look ☐    Nearly there ☐    Nailed it! ☐

**BIOLOGY 2.2.1**

# Organs and organ systems

## Organs

Organs are made of tissues. An organ, such as the stomach, may contain several different kinds of tissue.

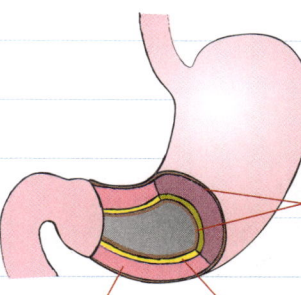

- epithelial tissue covers the outside and inside of the stomach
- muscular tissue churns the contents of the stomach
- glandular tissue produces digestive juices that contain enzymes

## Organ systems

An organ system is a group of organs that work together to perform a particular function in the body. For example, the organs of the digestive system work together to digest and take in (absorb) substances from the environment.

Other organ systems, such as the respiratory and excretory systems, exchange other substances between the body and the environment.

### EXAM ALERT!

Remember that the stomach produces acid and the liver produces alkaline bile.

Students have struggled with exam questions similar to this – **be prepared!**

## Worked example (target G-E)

Name the organs of the digestive system shown on the diagram and describe what each one does.
(3 marks)

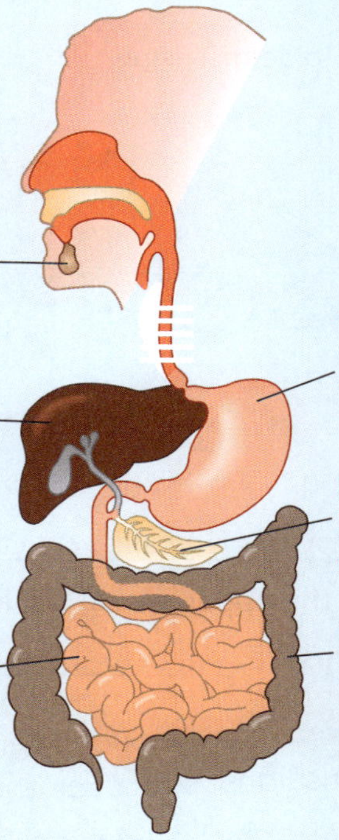

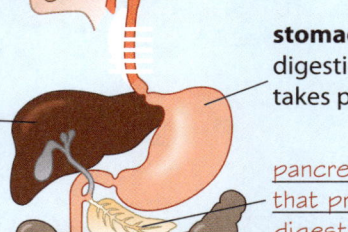

- salivary glands in mouth produce digestive juices
- liver – produces bile
- stomach – some digestion takes place here
- pancreas – a gland that produces digestive juices
- small intestine – digestion completed and absorption of soluble food
- large intestine – water absorbed from undigested food, leaving **faeces**

## Now try this

**(target G-E)**

1. Complete the sentences correctly. An organ may be made of several _____. For example, the stomach contains _____ that contracts and mixes the stomach contents. (2 marks)

**(target D-C)**

2. Name **two** organs of the digestive system that produce digestive juices. (2 marks)
3. Describe the function of the following organs in the digestive system:
   (a) stomach, (b) liver, (c) small intestine. (3 marks)

5

**BIOLOGY 2.2.2** | Had a look ☐    Nearly there ☐    Nailed it! ☐

# Plant organs

Plants have organs too.

Some plant organs are shown in the diagram. Each plant organ is made up of several different plant tissues. The tissues work together so that the organ can carry out its function well.

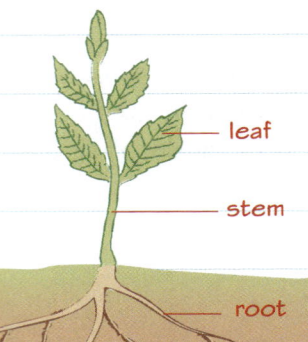

- leaf
- stem
- root

## Worked example (D-C)

The diagram shows some of the tissues in a plant leaf. Describe the function of each of these tissues.
*(3 marks)*

Labels: mesophyll tissue, epidermal tissue, xylem tissue, phloem tissue

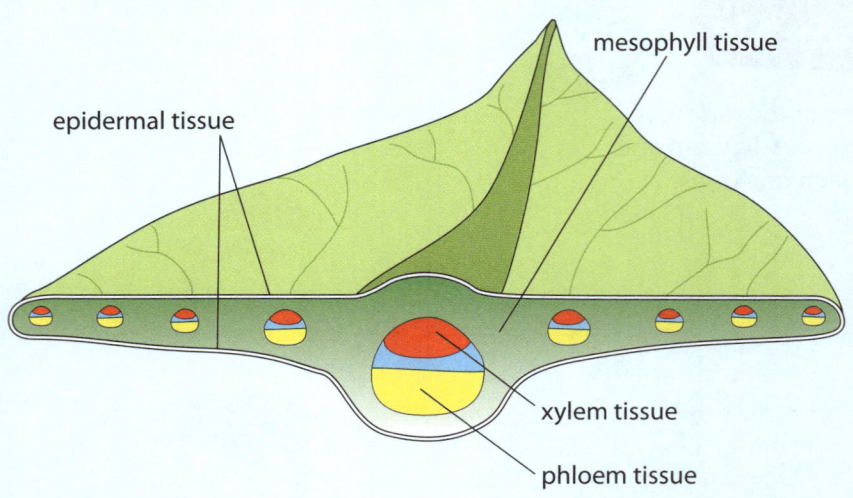

Epidermal tissue: <u>Covers the surface of the leaf.</u>
Mesophyll tissue in the upper part of the leaf: <u>Carries out photosynthesis.</u>
Xylem and phloem tissue: <u>Transport substances around the plant.</u>

> Epidermal tissue, xylem and phloem tissue carry out the same functions wherever they are in the plant.
> Mesophyll tissue only carries out photosynthesis when it includes cells that contain chlorophyll.

## Now try this

**1** (G-E) A leaf is a plant organ. Name **one** other plant organ. *(1 mark)*

**2** Name **two** tissues found in a plant leaf. *(2 marks)*

**3** (D-C) Describe the function of the tissues that you named in Question 2. *(2 marks)*

6

Had a look ☐  Nearly there ☐  Nailed it! ☐  **BIOLOGY 2.3.1**

# Photosynthesis

PHOTOSYNTHESIS is the process that plants use to make their own food. This equation summarises what happens in photosynthesis.

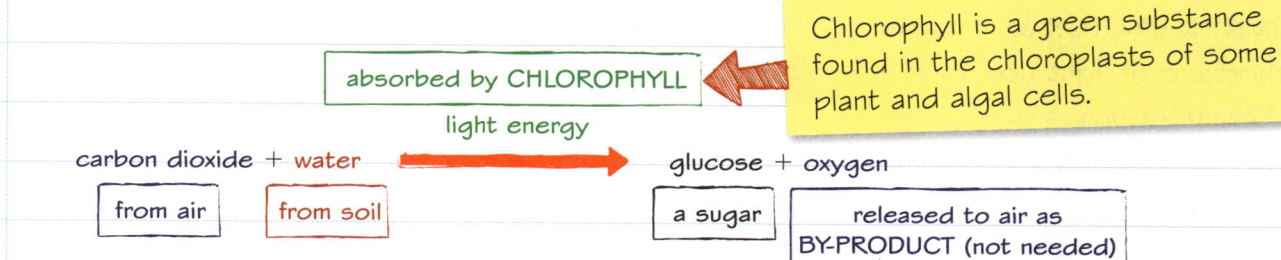

$$\text{carbon dioxide (from air)} + \text{water (from soil)} \xrightarrow[\text{absorbed by CHLOROPHYLL}]{\text{light energy}} \text{glucose (a sugar)} + \text{oxygen (released to air as BY-PRODUCT (not needed))}$$

Chlorophyll is a green substance found in the chloroplasts of some plant and algal cells.

**USES FOR GLUCOSE IN PLANTS AND ALGAE**
- converted to insoluble starch for storage
- converted to fat or oil for storage
- broken down to release energy in respiration
- converted to protein
- converted to cellulose, to strengthen cell walls

Don't forget, plants need to absorb nitrate ions from the soil so they can make proteins by combining the ions with glucose.

## Worked example (target D–C)

Iodine solution turns from brown to blue-black in the presence of starch. The diagram shows a variegated leaf before and after staining with iodine solution. Explain the results shown in the diagram. *(3 marks)*

- cells with no chlorophyll
- cells with chlorophyll
- before staining with iodine
- after staining with iodine

The staining shows that only the green areas which contain chlorophyll turned black, showing the presence of starch.

Starch is formed from glucose made during photosynthesis. Only areas that contain chlorophyll can capture light and photosynthesise to make glucose.

## Now try this

**(target G–E)**
1. Where does the water used by a plant for photosynthesis come from? *(1 mark)*
2. State **two** uses of glucose in a plant. *(2 marks)*

**(target D–C)**
3. Describe how plants use the nitrate ions that they absorb from the soil. *(2 marks)*

# Limiting factors

Light intensity, carbon dioxide availability and temperature affect the RATE OF PHOTOSYNTHESIS. Any one of these may be the LIMITING FACTOR at any time:
- a shortage of light (low light intensity)
- low temperature
- a shortage of carbon dioxide.

**Practical note:** You can measure the effect of different factors on the rate of photosynthesis by measuring the rate at which oxygen is produced by plant or algal cells. Remember that oxygen is a by-product of photosynthesis.

## Worked example

The graph shows the effect of changing light intensity on the rate of photosynthesis. Explain the shape of the graph at points A and B.
(4 marks)

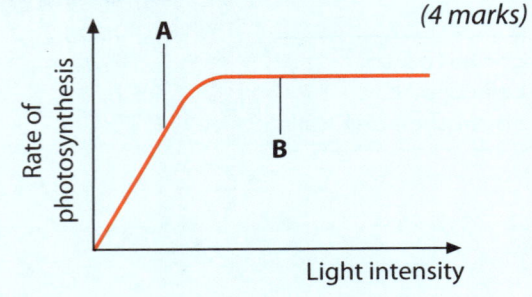

At A, the rate of photosynthesis increases as light intensity increases. This is because light intensity is limiting the rate of photosynthesis. At B, increasing the light intensity has no effect on the rate of photosynthesis, so another factor is limiting, such as carbon dioxide availability or temperature.

Increasing carbon dioxide availability, while keeping all other factors constant, will produce a graph similar to this.

## Limiting factors in greenhouses

Some crops, such as tomatoes, can be grown in greenhouses.

| Environment in greenhouse changed by: | → | Plants photosynthesise faster and make more food. | → | Plants grow faster and produce a greater crop yield. | → | Plant grower earns more money selling the crop. |

Environment in greenhouse changed by:
- keeping lights on when outside is dull or dark
- heating the air when it is cold
- adding carbon dioxide to air.

## Now try this

1. Describe **one** way of increasing the rate of photosynthesis in a plant. (1 mark)

2. On a warm sunny day, a boy sees many bubbles of gas rising from the plants growing at the bottom of his pond. The next day is warm but cloudy. He looks at the pond but does not see many bubbles.

    (a) Explain which gas is in the bubbles. (2 marks)

    (b) Explain the difference in the rate of bubble production on the two days. (2 marks)

Had a look ☐   Nearly there ☐   Nailed it! ☐   **BIOLOGY**

# Biology six mark question 1

There will be one 6 mark question on your exam paper, which will be marked for *quality of written communication* as well as scientific knowledge. This means that you need to apply your scientific knowledge, present your answer in a logical and organised way, and make sure that your spelling, grammar and punctuation are as good as you can make them.

## Worked example

In 2010, a grower set up a large greenhouse to grow cucumbers to sell. In 2011, the only change the grower made to the greenhouse was to add lights, which she kept on all night. She grew the same number of plants as in 2010. The table shows the record of her crop yield in the two years.

| Year | Yield in kilograms |
|------|--------------------|
| 2010 | 43.5               |
| 2011 | 78.2               |

Explain the advantages and disadvantages of adjusting the environment inside a greenhouse. *(6 marks)*

*The plants that grew in 2011 produced 78.2 − 43.5 = 29.7 tonnes more from the same number of plants. This is because they could grow all day and night, not just during the day.*

*The benefit of a bigger crop yield is that the grower will have more to sell and so earn more money.*

Cucumbers grown in a greenhouse.

### Advantages and disadvantages

This question asks for advantages and disadvantages. Make sure you give at least one example of each and explain why they are an advantage or a disadvantage.

This part of the answer should have mentioned photosynthesis, and that increasing light intensity increases the rate of photosynthesis. More photosynthesis means the plants can produce more food and so produce a greater yield of cucumbers.

The answer has not included a disadvantage. A better answer would have said that having the lights on all night uses electricity and so will cost the grower more money.

### EXAM ALERT!

Always plan what you are going to write for the 6 mark questions. You are given credit for a well-organised answer.

Students have struggled with exam questions similar to this – **be prepared!**

## Now try this

Describe the function of different cells, tissues and organs in the digestive system. *(6 marks)*

# BIOLOGY 2.4.1

Had a look ☐    Nearly there ☐    Nailed it! ☐

# Distribution of organisms

The DISTRIBUTION of a species is how the individuals of that species are spread out within an area.

PHYSICAL FACTORS of the environment may limit where organisms can live. This affects the distribution of the organisms.

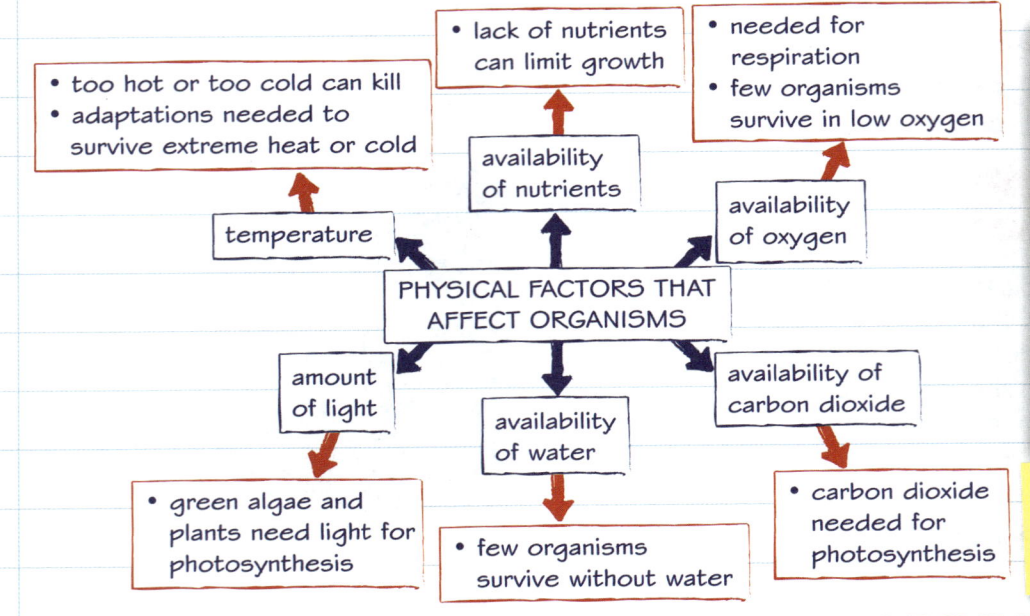

**PHYSICAL FACTORS THAT AFFECT ORGANISMS:**

- **temperature**
  - too hot or too cold can kill
  - adaptations needed to survive extreme heat or cold
- **availability of nutrients**
  - lack of nutrients can limit growth
- **availability of oxygen**
  - needed for respiration
  - few organisms survive in low oxygen
- **amount of light**
  - green algae and plants need light for photosynthesis
- **availability of water**
  - few organisms survive without water
- **availability of carbon dioxide**
  - carbon dioxide needed for photosynthesis

The distribution of buttercups depends on many physical factors.

## Worked example (target D–C)

**AQA SKILL: Interpret (Page 101)**

A class was studying the distribution of two buttercup species in the middle of a field. The diagram shows what they found.

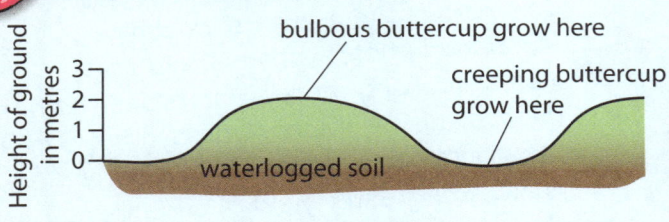

*Diagram: Height of ground in metres (0–3), showing bulbous buttercup grow here on top of ridge, creeping buttercup grow here in lower area, waterlogged soil at bottom.*

Draw a conclusion from this information about the effect of water on the distribution of these buttercup species. *(2 marks)*

Creeping buttercups can grow in the waterlogged conditions at the bottom of the ridge, but bulbous buttercups grow better where the ground is better drained at the top of the ridge.

You may be given information to interpret about the distribution of an organism. Remember the physical factors that might affect the organism.

## Now try this

**1** (target G–E) Name **two** physical factors that might affect where a plant lives. *(2 marks)*

**2** (target D–C) Very few organisms live in hot sandy desert areas. Suggest **two** physical factors that could be the reason for this. *(2 marks)*

**3** (target D–C) At the edge of a wood there are many low-growing plants. As you move deeper under the trees, there are fewer low-growing plants. Suggest a reason for this difference. *(2 marks)*

Had a look ☐   Nearly there ☐   Nailed it! ☐   **BIOLOGY 2.4.1**

# Sampling organisms

## Sampling with quadrats

When looking at the distribution of a species in an area, most areas are too large to count every individual organism. So we take SAMPLES and use them to draw conclusions about the whole area. Samples are often taken with QUADRATS.

- We can sample the DISTRIBUTION of plants or animals (how spread out they are) by counting the number of them in each quadrat.
- We can sample the ABUNDANCE of plants (how common they are) by measuring what percentage of a quadrat they fill.

We can compare the number of individuals of a species within quadrats in different areas to see which conditions they prefer to live in.

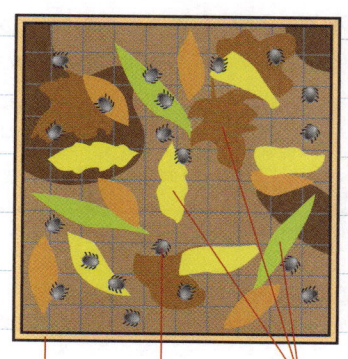

quadrat    woodlouse    leaf litter

A typical quadrat is often 50 × 50 cm square or 100 × 100 cm square, but they may be larger or smaller than this.

## Valid results

When sampling a large area, to get the best results we need to:

- sample randomly
- take several repeat samples and calculate the mean (average) value of those samples.

← This means not choosing where to place the quadrat, but using random numbers to decide where the quadrats are placed.

← Taking repeats and averaging the results helps to even out differences that occur by chance.

### Worked example (target D-C)

A student counted the number of daisies in seven randomly placed quadrats in a field. The table shows the results.

| Quadrat | 1 | 2 | 3 | 4 | 5 | 6 | 7 |
|---|---|---|---|---|---|---|---|
| Number of daisies | 3 | 0 | 3 | 1 | 2 | 3 | 2 |

Calculate the mean number of daisies in a quadrat. Show your working. *(2 marks)*

Total = 3 + 0 + 3 + 1 + 2 + 3 + 2 = 14

Mean = $\frac{14}{7}$ = 2 daisies

There are other kinds of averages:
- The **median** is the middle value when all the values are placed in order, i.e. 2 daisies (middle value of 0, 1, 2, **2**, 3, 3, 3).
- The **mode** is the value that occurs most commonly, i.e. 3 daisies (as 3 appears three times in the quadrat samples).

### Now try this

**(target G-E)**
1. What is a **quadrat**? *(1 mark)*

**(target D-C)**
2. Explain why random sampling and repeat sampling can help to produce good results when sampling a population using quadrats. *(2 marks)*

**(target D-C)**
3. The table shows the number of daisies counted in six quadrats placed in a different area. Calculate the mean number of daisies in one quadrat in this area. *(2 marks)*

| Quadrat | 1 | 2 | 3 | 4 | 5 | 6 |
|---|---|---|---|---|---|---|
| Number of daisies | 5 | 0 | 2 | 1 | 4 | 3 |

**BIOLOGY 2.4.1**  Had a look ☐   Nearly there ☐   Nailed it! ☐

# Transect sampling

A TRANSECT is used to sample the distribution of organisms as it changes between two neighbouring areas.

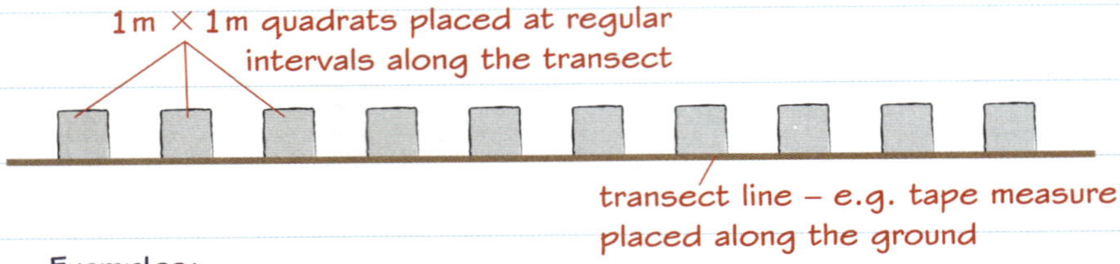

1m × 1m quadrats placed at regular intervals along the transect

transect line – e.g. tape measure placed along the ground

Examples:
pond → dry land
low tide on rocky shore → high tide

A transect can be used to study how this type of seaweed changes as you move up a shore.

Changes in physical factors (such as temperature, light intensity, trampling) are also recorded at each quadrat position. This means that it is easier to link a change in distribution with a change in a physical factor.

---

## Worked example  (target D–C)

**1 (a)** A transect of a rocky shore was carried out to investigate the distribution of different kinds of seaweed.
The shaded boxes in the table show where each kind was recorded in a quadrat.

| Seaweed | Distance from high water mark in m | | | | | | | | | |
|---|---|---|---|---|---|---|---|---|---|---|
| | 0 | 2 | 4 | 6 | 8 | 10 | 12 | 14 | 16 | 18 |
| | Time not covered by sea water in hours | | | | | | | | | |
| | 10 | 9 | 8 | 7 | 6 | 5 | 4 | 3 | 2 | 1 |
| Enteromorpha | | ▓ | ▓ | | | | | | | |
| Fucus vesiculosus | | | ▓ | ▓ | ▓ | ▓ | ▓ | | | |
| Fucus serratus | | | | | ▓ | ▓ | ▓ | ▓ | ▓ | |
| Corallina | | | | | | ▓ | ▓ | | | |

The longer a seaweed is in air, the more it dries out.
Identify the kind of seaweed that is least able to survive being dried out. Tick (✓) **one** box.  *(1 mark)*

| Seaweed | Tick (✓) |
|---|---|
| Enteromorpha | |
| Fucus vesiculosus | |
| Fucus serratus | ✓ |
| Corallina | |

**(b)** Explain how the seaweed study in question 1 could have been improved so that you could be more certain that the results were reproducible. *(2 marks)*

Repeating the transects several times and comparing the results for each transect would help to average out any random variation.

---

## Now try this

**(target G–E)**

**1** Choose the correct words from the box to complete the sentences that describe how a transect is used.   | distribution   samples   species   variation |

A transect is a series of _____ taken at regular intervals. This can show how the _____ of organisms changes from one area to another. *(2 marks)*

**(target D–C)**

**2** Use the results in the table above to explain which seaweed is most tolerant of being dried out. *(2 marks)*

Had a look ☐    Nearly there ☐    Nailed it! ☐    **BIOLOGY 2.5.1**

# Proteins

There are many different kinds of PROTEINS in the body.

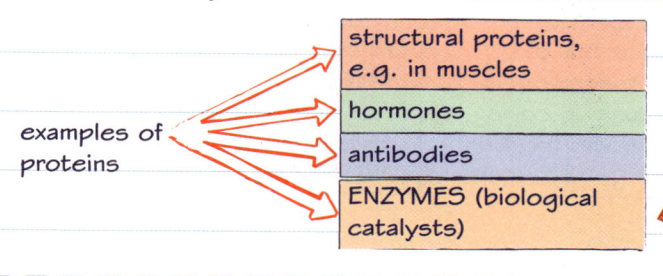

examples of proteins:
- structural proteins, e.g. in muscles
- hormones
- antibodies
- ENZYMES (biological catalysts)

A **catalyst** changes the rate of a reaction, often increasing the rate. Enzymes help many reactions in the body to work faster.

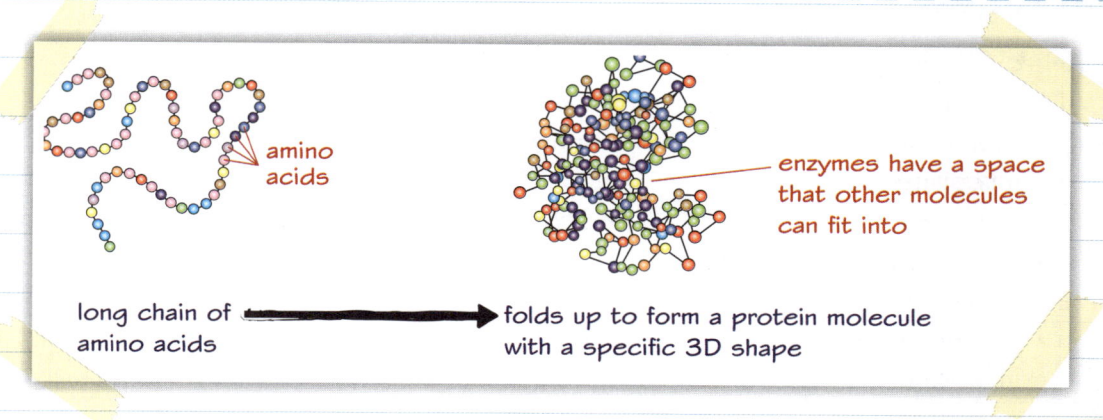

long chain of amino acids → folds up to form a protein molecule with a specific 3D shape

enzymes have a space that other molecules can fit into

The shape of an enzyme is important. If the shape changes, it cannot work as well as a catalyst. We say that the enzyme has been **denatured**.

## Worked example (target G-E)

Complete the sentences with words from the box to explain how enzyme function can be affected by different factors.

| amino acids   shape   pH   concentration |   (2 marks)

A high temperature changes the <u>shape</u> of an enzyme so it does not work so well.

Different enzymes work better at high or low <u>pH</u>.

### EXAM ALERT!

Remember that enzymes are molecules and are not living, so they cannot be killed. When they are damaged and stop working, they are said to be denatured.

Students have struggled with questions like this in recent exams – **be prepared!**

## Now try this

**1** (target G-E) Select **one** word from the list to answer this question.

| carbohydrate   protein   fat |

What kind of molecule is an enzyme?
(1 mark)

**2** (target G-E) Name **two** uses of proteins in the human body, other than as enzymes.
(2 marks)

**3** (target D-C) The graph shows the rate of a reaction catalysed by an enzyme at different temperatures. Explain the shape of the graph above 40 °C.
(2 marks)

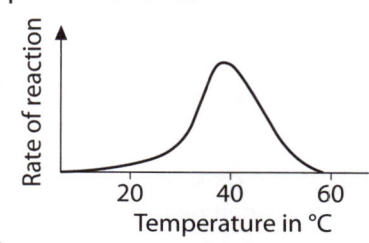

13

**BIOLOGY 2.5.2**   Had a look ☐   Nearly there ☐   Nailed it! ☐

# Digestive enzymes

Some enzymes work outside body cells, such as in the gut.

| Digestive enzymes produced by specialised cells in salivary glands, stomach, pancreas, and in the lining of the gut. | → | Enzymes pass out of gland cells (secreted) into gut. Enzymes come into contact with food molecules. | → | Enzymes catalyse breakdown of large food molecules into smaller molecules (DIGESTION). |

## Different digestive enzymes

| Enzyme | Produced by ... | Place of action | Breaks down ... |
|---|---|---|---|
| amylase | • salivary glands<br>• pancreas and small intestine | • mouth<br>• small intestine | starch to sugars |
| proteases | • stomach<br>• pancreas and small intestine | • stomach<br>• small intestine | proteins to amino acids |
| lipases | • pancreas and small intestine | • small intestine | lipids (fats and oils) to fatty acids and glycerol |

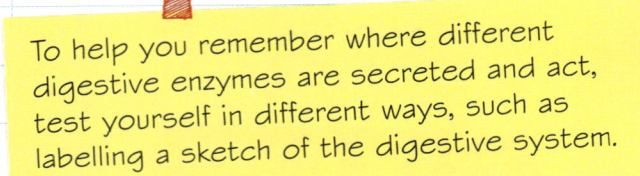

To help you remember where different digestive enzymes are secreted and act, test yourself in different ways, such as labelling a sketch of the digestive system.

### Worked example  (target D-C)

(a) State where bile is produced and stored before it enters the small intestine.
*(2 marks)*

Bile is produced in the liver and stored in the gall bladder until it is needed.

(b) Explain the importance of bile in digestion.
*(2 marks)*

Bile neutralises the acid from the stomach, making the contents of the small intestine more alkaline. The enzymes of the small intestine work better in alkaline conditions.

### Stomach acid

Cells lining the stomach release hydrochloric acid into the food in the stomach.

Enzymes in the stomach work best when the pH is acidic.

## Now try this

**1** (target G-E)
(a) Which type of enzyme breaks down starch? *(1 mark)*
(b) What is starch broken down to by this enzyme? *(1 mark)*
(c) Name **one** part of the body where this enzyme is produced. *(1 mark)*

**2** (target D-C) State the role of enzymes in the digestion of food in the gut. *(1 mark)*

Had a look ☐   Nearly there ☐   Nailed it! ☐

**BIOLOGY 2.5.2**

# Microbial enzymes

Some microorganisms produce enzymes, which then pass out of the cell into the surrounding environment. We use some of these enzymes in the home and in industry.

## Uses of enzymes

- **LIPASES** – fat-digesting enzymes
- **PROTEASES** – protein-digesting enzymes
- **CARBOHYDRASES** – carbohydrate-digesting enzymes
- **ISOMERASE enzyme** – converts glucose syrup to fructose syrup

↓

- **BIOLOGICAL DETERGENTS** clean better at low temperatures than detergents with no enzymes
- **BABY FOOD** enzymes 'pre-digest' proteins so they are easier for babies to digest
- convert starch (not very useful) to sugar syrup (used in many foods)
- fructose is much sweeter than glucose, so it is used in smaller amounts in **SLIMMING FOODS**

enzymes used in the home | enzymes used in industry

## Worked example  *target D-C*

**AQA SKILL: Interpret  Page 101**

The table shows the results from different detergents on the same cleaning test. Do the results support manufacturer claims that biological detergents give better cleaning than those without enzymes? Explain your answer. *(2 marks)*

**Detergent performance based on stain removal, whiteness and limit to colour fading**

|  | biological | non-biological |
|---|---|---|
| least effective brand | 58% | 41% |
| most effective brand | 81% | 70% |

The results do support the claim, because performance was better for biological detergents than non-biological at both ends of the range of effectiveness.

## Enzymes in industry

**Advantages:**
- ✓ Bring about reactions at lower temperatures and pressures.
- ✓ Avoids need for expensive equipment that takes a lot of energy to run.

**Disadvantages:**
- ✗ Enzymes denature if the temperature is too high.
- ✗ Many enzymes are costly to produce.

## Now try this

*target G-E*
1. Give **two** examples of the use of enzymes. *(2 marks)*

*target D-C*
2. Enzymes are used to break down wood that will be used to make paper. The temperature is controlled in this process so that the enzymes are not denatured.
   (a) State how denaturing affects an enzyme. *(1 mark)*
   (b) Describe the impact that denaturing would have on the process. *(2 marks)*

**BIOLOGY 2.6.1** | Had a look ☐ | Nearly there ☐ | Nailed it! ☐

# Aerobic respiration

The chemical reactions inside cells, including those of aerobic respiration, are controlled by enzymes.

AEROBIC RESPIRATION is a series of chemical reactions that take place mostly inside mitochondria in the cell.

Mitochondria is pronounced 'my-toe-**con**-dree-a'.

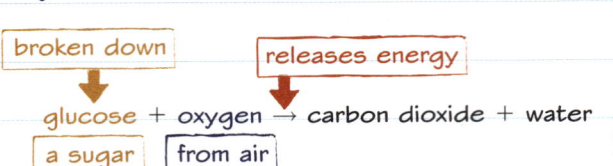

glucose (a sugar, broken down) + oxygen (from air) → carbon dioxide + water (releases energy)

Aerobic means 'needs air'.

### EXAM ALERT!

Make sure you use the phrase 'releases energy' when describing the function of respiration.

Students have struggled with this topic in the past – **be prepared!**

## Worked example (target G-E)

Tick (✓) the box that shows the correct statement about aerobic respiration. *(1 mark)*

| Statement | Tick (✓) |
|---|---|
| Aerobic respiration only takes place during the day in plants and animals. | |
| Aerobic respiration only takes place in plants and animals when there is light. | |
| Aerobic respiration takes place all the time in plants and animals. | ✓ |

## Use of energy from respiration

| | | |
|---|---|---|
| animals | to build larger molecules from smaller ones e.g. proteins from amino acids, large carbohydrates (e.g. starch, glycogen) from small sugars (e.g. glucose), fats from fatty acids and glycerol | enables muscles to contract |
| birds and mammals | also used to maintain steady body temperature in colder surroundings | |
| plants | to build larger molecules from smaller ones e.g. from sugars, nitrates and other nutrients into amino acids → used to make proteins | |

## Now try this

**(target G-E)** 1. State **one** use of the energy released from respiration in a plant. *(1 mark)*

2. In which of the following cell structures does aerobic respiration mainly take place: chloroplasts, cytoplasm, mitochondria, nucleus? *(1 mark)*

**(target D-C)** 3. Define the term **aerobic respiration**. *(2 marks)*

Had a look ☐    Nearly there ☐    Nailed it! ☐    **BIOLOGY 2.6.1**

# The effect of exercise

During exercise ...

- rate of breathing increases
- depth of breathing increases

→

- more oxygen gets into blood from the lungs
- more carbon dioxide removed from body

→

- more oxygen reaches muscles
- more carbon dioxide removed from muscles
- more glucose reaches muscles

- heart rate increases

→

- blood flows more quickly around body, including to muscles

glucose in blood comes from:
- digested food
- muscle stores of GLYCOGEN – glycogen is converted back to glucose during exercise

Changes inside the body during exercise increase body temperature and the pH of cells (because carbon dioxide dissolves to form acidic solutions). Too great a change can reduce how well enzymes work.

---

## Worked example    target D–C

**AQA SKILL Interpret Page 101**

The graph shows changes to the body during exercise.

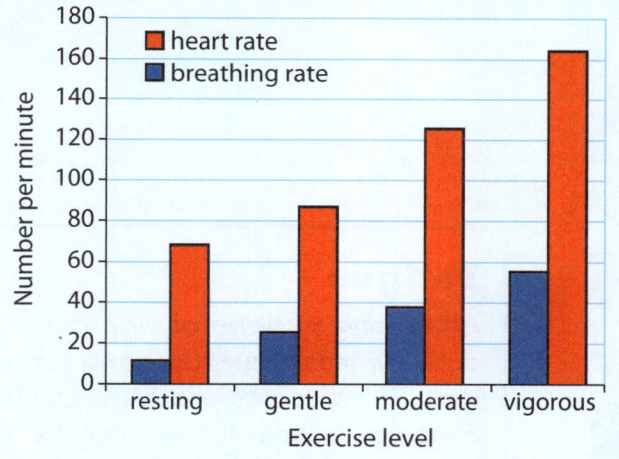

[Bar chart: Number per minute (0–180) vs Exercise level (resting, gentle, moderate, vigorous). Heart rate bars: ~68, ~88, ~125, ~165. Breathing rate bars: ~12, ~25, ~38, ~55.]

Explain the shape of the bar chart.    *(3 marks)*

The graph shows that both heart rate and breathing rate increase as the level of exercise increases. These changes mean that more oxygen and glucose get to the muscles so that they can contract faster. The changes also remove the extra carbon dioxide produced during exercise.

---

## Now try this

**target G–E**

1  Give **two** changes that happen in the body during exercise.    *(2 marks)*

**target D–C**

2  Why do muscles need more oxygen and glucose during exercise?    *(2 marks)*

3  Most of the glucose used by muscle cells during exercise comes from digested food. Where does the rest come from?    *(2 marks)*

# BIOLOGY 2.6.2

Had a look ☐ Nearly there ☐ Nailed it! ☐

# Anaerobic respiration

During exercise, some of the energy needed by muscles for contraction may come from ANAEROBIC RESPIRATION.

- anaerobic respiration = incomplete breakdown of glucose to release energy
  - doesn't use oxygen → can supply energy to muscles when there is not enough oxygen for aerobic respiration
  - in muscle cells, produces lactic acid → blood flowing through muscles then removes the lactic acid

## Worked example (target G-E)

The graph shows the concentration of lactic acid in the blood related to exercise level.

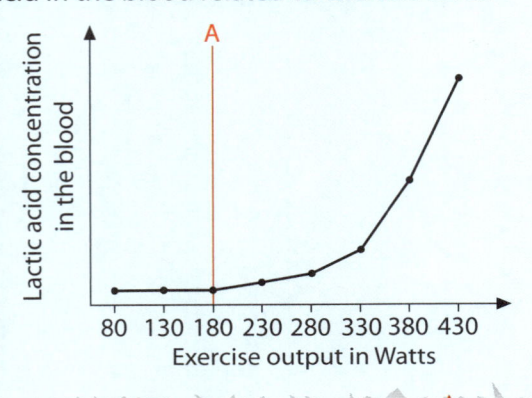

[Graph: Lactic acid concentration in the blood vs Exercise output in Watts (80, 130, 180, 230, 280, 330, 380, 430). Point A marked at 180.]

Complete the sentences to describe what the graph shows. *(2 marks)*

As exercise level increases up to point A, blood lactic acid concentration <u>stays the same</u>.

As exercise level increases beyond point A, blood lactic acid concentration <u>increases</u>.

## EXAM ALERT!

Remember the connection between lactic acid production in cells and anaerobic respiration.

Students have struggled with exam questions similar to this – **be prepared!**

## Fatigue

After long periods of vigorous activity, muscles stop contracting well. The muscles are FATIGUED. One cause of muscle fatigue may be the build-up of lactic acid in the muscles.

## Now try this

**1** (target G-E) Which form of respiration does not need oxygen? *(1 mark)*

**2** (target D-C) Look at the graph above. Suggest why the shape of the graph changes at point A. *(2 marks)*

**3** Using your knowledge of lactic acid, explain why it takes a few minutes for muscles to recover after vigorous activity. *(2 marks)*

Had a look ☐   Nearly there ☐   Nailed it! ☐          **BIOLOGY**

# Biology six mark question 2

There will be one 6 mark question on your exam paper, which will be marked for *quality of written communication* as well as scientific knowledge. This means that you need to apply your scientific knowledge, present your answer in a logical and organised way, and make sure that your spelling, grammar and punctuation are as good as you can make them.

## Worked example

Explain why the stomach secretes enzymes and hydrochloric acid, and bile is released into the small intestine, during the digestion of food. *(6 marks)*

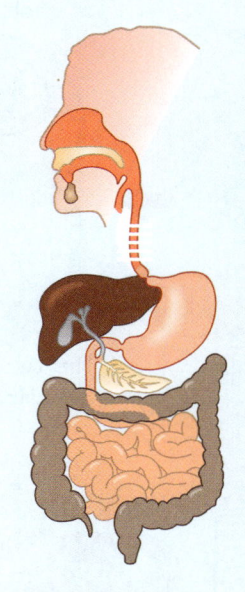

Food is broken down by enzymes. Enzymes need the right conditions to work well.

Hydrochloric acid is released into the food in the stomach. It makes the food acidic, so the protease enzymes there work better.

Bile is made in the liver and stored in the gall bladder. It is released into the small intestine where it makes the food alkaline, so that the protease, lipase and amylase enzymes there work better.

### Explain

The command word in this question is 'explain'. This means that you need to say what is happening and why.

The first part of the answer is not clear enough and needs to say that different pH levels can change the shape of an enzyme and so change how well it works. It could also have said that some enzymes work better at high pH and others at low pH.

The question didn't ask about where bile was made and stored, so this part of the answer is wasted.
This part of the answer would have been better if it explained that protease enzymes break down proteins to amino acids, lipase enzymes break down fats and oils to fatty acids and glycerol, and amylase breaks down starch to sugars. The answer could also explain that the breakdown of large food molecules to small soluble molecules makes it possible for the body to absorb nutrients from food in the gut.

## Now try this

Explain the changes that occur in the human body during exercise, including the need for both aerobic and anaerobic respiration.
*(6 marks)*

**BIOLOGY 2.7.1** | Had a look ☐   Nearly there ☐   Nailed it! ☐

# Mitosis

The CHROMOSOMES in the nucleus of a body cell contain the genetic information (GENES) of the cell. The chromosomes of body cells come in pairs.

MITOSIS is one kind of cell division. It occurs:
- during growth – to produce more body cells
- to produce replacement cells – when body cells are damaged
- during asexual reproduction.

## Body cells divide by mitosis

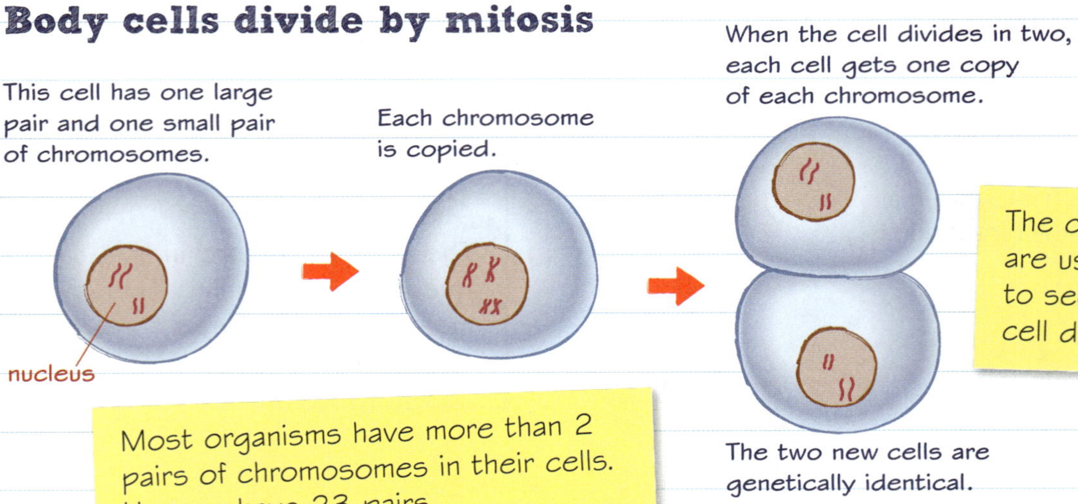

This cell has one large pair and one small pair of chromosomes.

Each chromosome is copied.

When the cell divides in two, each cell gets one copy of each chromosome.

nucleus

The chromosomes are usually not easy to see except during cell division.

Most organisms have more than 2 pairs of chromosomes in their cells. Humans have 23 pairs.

The two new cells are genetically identical.

### Asexual reproduction
Some organisms can produce new individuals *without* fertilisation. This is ASEXUAL reproduction.

Each new individual is formed from the division of a body cell of *one* parent.

### Worked example (target G-E)

Complete the sentences about asexual reproduction. *(2 marks)*

The cells of offspring produced by asexual reproduction contain the same <u>alleles</u> as the cells of the parent. This means they are genetically <u>identical</u>.

An **allele** is one form of a gene.

### EXAM ALERT!
Remember that cells made by mitosis are identical to each other and to the parent cell.

Students have struggled with exam questions similar to this – **be prepared!**

## Now try this

**target G-E**
1. Give **one** example of when mitosis occurs. *(1 mark)*
2. How many parents does an individual produced by asexual reproduction have? *(1 mark)*

**target D-C**
3. Explain why all the body cells of an organism are genetically identical. *(2 marks)*

Had a look ☐  Nearly there ☐  Nailed it! ☐

**BIOLOGY 2.7.1**

# Sexual reproduction

## Chromosome sets
- Body cells contain two sets of chromosomes (the two sets form pairs during mitosis).
- SEX CELLS (GAMETES) contain one set of chromosomes.

Gametes are produced from body cells by a kind of cell division called MEIOSIS.

## Human reproductive organs
Gametes are formed in REPRODUCTIVE ORGANS.

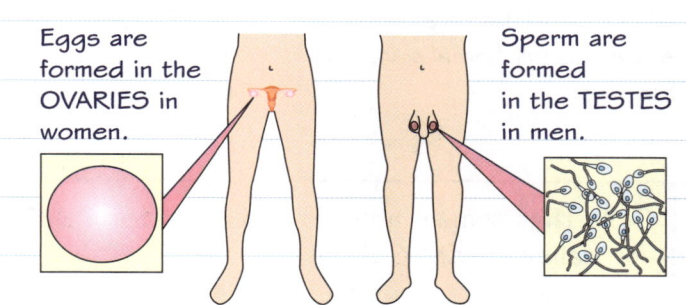

Eggs are formed in the OVARIES in women.

Sperm are formed in the TESTES in men.

## Sexual reproduction
In SEXUAL REPRODUCTION, a male gamete joins with a female gamete.

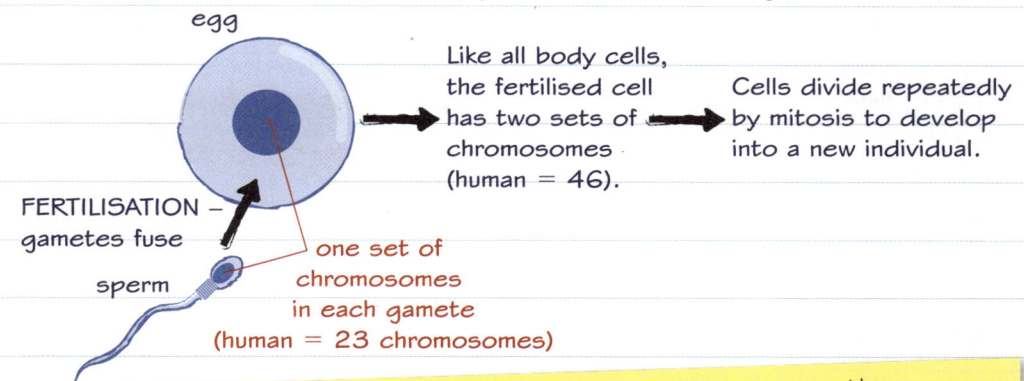

FERTILISATION – gametes fuse

one set of chromosomes in each gamete (human = 23 chromosomes)

Like all body cells, the fertilised cell has two sets of chromosomes (human = 46).

Cells divide repeatedly by mitosis to develop into a new individual.

Sexual reproduction produces **variation** in the offspring, as the fertilised cell contains one set of chromosomes from each parent. So one of each pair of alleles in each body cell comes from each parent.

## Sex chromosomes
In human body cells, one of the 23 pairs of chromosomes carries the genes that determine sex. They are called the SEX CHROMOSOMES.

### Worked example (target D-C)

Complete the sentences. *(4 marks)*

The sex chromosomes of a woman are <u>XX</u>.
The sex chromosomes of a man are <u>XY</u>.
The sex chromosome in a human egg is <u>X</u>.
The sex chromosome in a human sperm can be <u>X</u> or <u>Y</u>.

### Now try this

**target G-E**

1. Which form of cell division produces gametes? *(1 mark)*
2. In humans, in which sex are the pair of sex chromosomes different? *(1 mark)*

**target D-C**

3. Explain how sexual reproduction produces variation in offspring. *(2 marks)*

21

**BIOLOGY 2.7.1**

Had a look ☐   Nearly there ☐   Nailed it! ☐

# Stem cells

## Cell differentiation

Most cells in growing organisms DIFFERENTIATE into cells that are specialised for a particular function.

animals → most cells differentiate at an early stage → in mature animals, cell division is mainly for repair and replacement of cells

plants → many cells are able to divide and differentiate into specialised cells throughout life

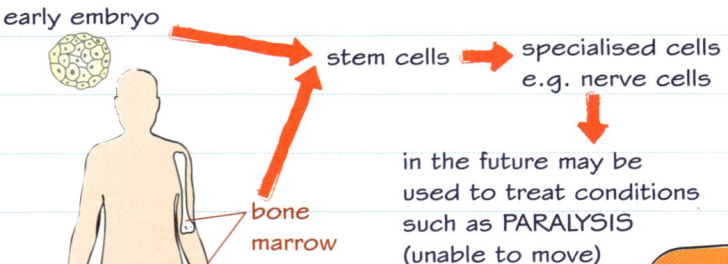

---

Cells that remain able to divide to form different specialised cells are called STEM CELLS.

early embryo → stem cells → specialised cells e.g. nerve cells

bone marrow

in the future may be used to treat conditions such as PARALYSIS (unable to move)

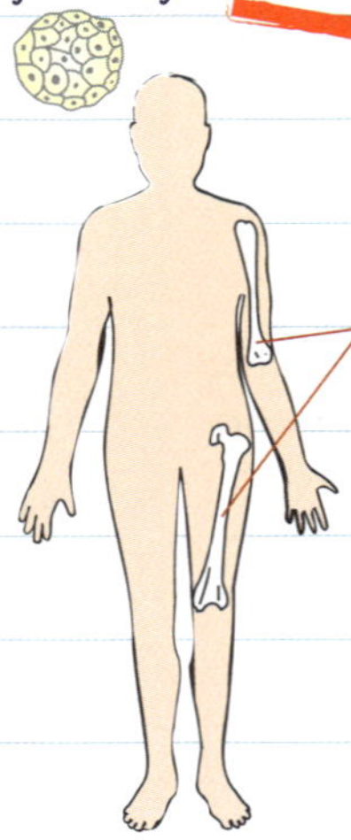

Scientists can make human stem cells differentiate into many kinds of specialised cell.

### EXAM ALERT!

Be prepared in a longer answer question to give your opinion on the use of stem cells, and to justify your opinion.

Students have struggled with exam questions similar to this – **be prepared!**

## Worked example (target G-E)

Stem cells from early embryos may be used in research to find new treatments for human diseases. Tick (✓) **two** advantages and **two** disadvantages of this. (4 marks)

| | Advantage Tick (✓) | Disadvantage Tick (✓) |
|---|---|---|
| This destroys the embryo, which is destroying a potential life. | | ✓ |
| Stem cells may change into cancer cells and cause more disease. | | ✓ |
| This may be the quickest way to develop a new treatment for a human disease. | ✓ | |
| New stem cell research does not need embryos to produce stem cells. | | |
| Stem cells are usually taken from embryos left over from fertility treatments. | ✓ | |

## Now try this

1 Name **two** sources of stem cells. (2 marks) *(target G-E)*

2 Define the term **stem cell**. (1 mark) *(target D-C)*

3 Describe the difference between cell differentiation in plants and cell differentiation in animals. (2 marks)

Had a look ☐    Nearly there ☐    Nailed it! ☐    **BIOLOGY 2.7.2**

# Genes and alleles

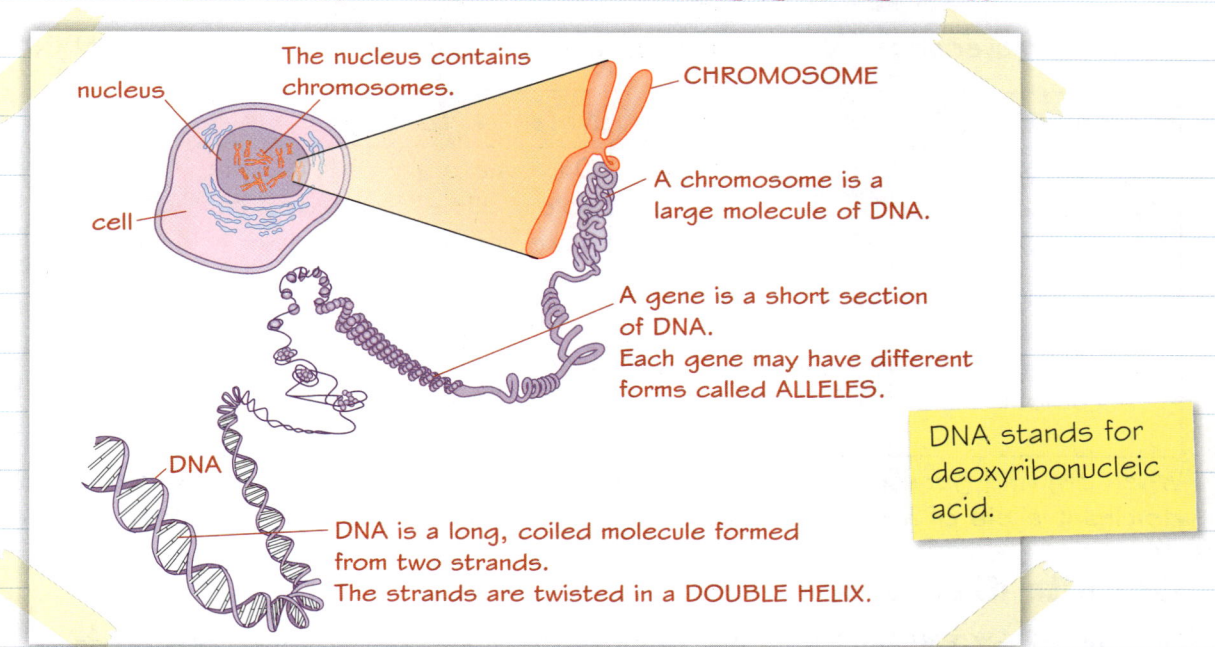

- nucleus
- The nucleus contains chromosomes.
- CHROMOSOME
- cell
- A chromosome is a large molecule of DNA.
- A gene is a short section of DNA. Each gene may have different forms called ALLELES.
- DNA
- DNA is a long, coiled molecule formed from two strands. The strands are twisted in a DOUBLE HELIX.

DNA stands for deoxyribonucleic acid.

## Alleles

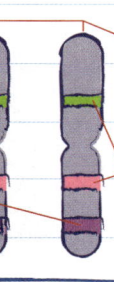

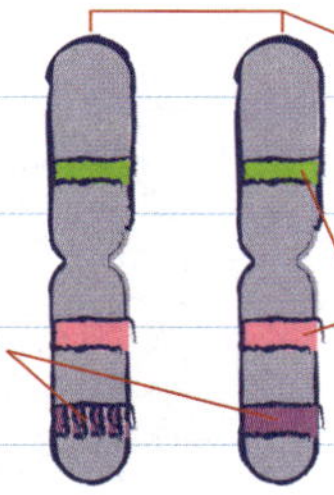

- Chromosomes of a pair are the same size and have the same genes in the same order.
- These genes have the same allele on both chromosomes.
- This gene has different alleles on the two chromosomes.

Remember that chromosomes in body cells come in pairs.

### Worked example (target D–C)

The diagram shows part of the DNA fingerprints of four people. Which **two** of these people are identical twins? Explain your answer. *(2 marks)*

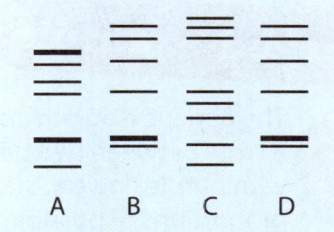

B and D are identical twins because they have identical DNA. Everybody else has unique DNA, so that they differ from each other.

A   B   C   D

### Now try this

1. **(target G–E)** Choose the right definition from the list for each of these words:
   (a) DNA;   (b) gene.   *(2 marks)*
   Definitions
   (i) A large molecule of DNA.
   (ii) A small section of DNA.
   (iii) A large molecule with a double helix structure.

2. **(target D–C)** Police investigators often take samples of blood or other tissues at crime scenes for making DNA fingerprints. Explain how this can help their investigation of the crime. *(2 marks)*

23

**BIOLOGY 2.7.2** | Had a look ☐  Nearly there ☐  Nailed it! ☐

# Genetic diagrams

Some characteristics are controlled by a single gene. This is MONOHYBRID INHERITANCE.

| Characteristic | Alleles | Note |
|---|---|---|
| purple flower colour | R R or R r | Only one copy of R (purple colour allele) is needed to make the flower purple. R is DOMINANT to r. |
| white flower colour | only r r | Both alleles must be r (white colour allele) to make the flower white. r is RECESSIVE to R. |

*Flower colour in peas is controlled by a single gene that has different alleles.*

*Remember that every individual has two alleles for most genes.*

When drawing genetic diagrams or Punnett squares a capital letter is used for the dominant allele of a gene, and a small letter for the recessive allele of that gene.

## Genetic diagram

We can use a GENETIC DIAGRAM to show the possible outcomes of a cross between two individuals.

*AQA SKILL: Draw — Page 101*

parent plants: flower R r  ×  flower R r
pollen grains: R, r   egg cells: R, r
different possible gametes
possible combinations
offspring: RR, Rr, Rr, rr

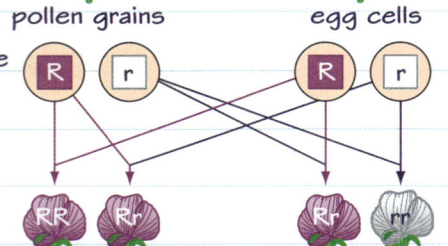

Half the gametes contain one allele. the other half contain the other allele.

*Remember that a genetic diagram only shows possible outcomes of a cross, not the actual outcome.*

## Worked example (target D–C)

*AQA SKILL: Predict — Page 101*

The genetic diagram above shows a cross between two pea plants with purple flowers. State the proportions of possible outcomes of alleles and characteristics for this cross. *(2 marks)*

The proportions of possible allele combinations are: 1 RR to 2 Rr to 1 rr.
The proportions of possible characteristics are: 3 purple flower colour to 1 white flower colour.

*This answer needs to describe the alleles as well as the characteristics in the offspring.*

## Now try this

**1** (target G–E) Choose the correct word to complete the sentence.

| dominant | gamete | recessive |

An allele that controls the development of a characteristic only if there are two copies present is a _____ allele. *(1 mark)*

**2** (target D–C) Look at the genetic diagram above. Explain how two pea plants with purple flowers can produce a pea plant that has white flowers. *(3 marks)*

Had a look ☐    Nearly there ☐    Nailed it! ☐

**BIOLOGY 2.7.2**

# Mendel's work

Gregor Mendel studied the inheritance of many characteristics in pea plants.

## Mendel's methods

Gregor Mendel carried out his work scientifically.

- He spent several years producing plants that were PURE-BREEDING (produced the same characteristic every time when bred with each other) – he used these as his parent plants in his experiments.
- He made the crosses by hand so he could be certain which parent plants produced which offspring.
- He repeated each test hundreds of times.

> Mendel published his work in 1865. Few people read it.
>
> ↓
>
> Mendel died in 1884.
>
> ↓
>
> Later work by other scientists linked Mendel's 'inherited factors' to genes and chromosomes.

## Mendel's crosses

parents: plant with green pods × plant with yellow pods
↓
first generation: all plants had green pods – green is dominant, yellow is recessive → plants with green pods

first generation plants crossed with other first generation plants
↓
second generation: 3 plants green to 1 plant yellow → plants with green pods / plants with yellow pods

### Mendel's results

Mendel was the first person to show that in the second generation, there were about 3 times more plants with the dominant characteristic than plants with the recessive characteristic.

## Worked example (D-C)

Mendel concluded from his experiments that characteristics are caused by 'separately inherited factors'. Use the diagram above to help you explain Mendel's conclusion. *(2 marks)*

He showed that some characteristics of parent plants seem to disappear in the first generation (e.g. yellow pod), but reappear in the second generation. So the factors that cause the colours must be kept separate even in green 1st generation plants.

## Now try this

1. (G-E) Give **one** reason why the importance of Mendel's work wasn't recognised until after his death. *(1 mark)*

2. (D-C) Why did repeating the crosses hundreds of times help to show that Mendel's conclusion was valid? *(2 marks)*

# Punnett squares

A genetic cross can also be described using a PUNNETT SQUARE.

This Punnett square shows the same information as the genetic diagram on page 24. The coloured squares show the alleles of the possible offspring.

R is the dominant allele for purple-coloured flowers.

r is the recessive allele for white-coloured flowers.

This shows that the possible outcomes are:
- a chance of 1 in 4 for RR
- a chance of 2 in 4 for Rr
- a chance of 1 in 4 for rr
- a chance of 3 in 4 for purple colour
- a chance of 1 in 4 for white colour.

|  |  | parent Rr pollen grains | |
|---|---|---|---|
|  |  | R | r |
| parent Rr egg cells | R | RR | Rr |
|  | r | Rr | rr |

— possible allele combinations of offspring

## Polydactyly

Some disorders are caused by genes. This means they can be INHERITED.

POLYDACTYLY is a condition of having more than the usual number of five toes on a foot or five fingers on a hand.

One type of polydactyly is caused by a dominant allele. So it can be inherited when only one parent has the allele.

In this table we use D for the polydactyly allele, and d for the allele that produces the usual number of fingers and toes:

| Alleles | Number of fingers/toes |
|---|---|
| DD | polydactyly |
| Dd | polydactyly |
| dd | usual number |

### Worked example (target D-C)

**AQA SKILL Predict Page 101**

This Punnett square shows a cross between a father who has one polydactyly allele (Dd) and a mother who does not have a polydactyly allele (dd). Complete the square to show all the possible combinations of alleles their children could have. *(3 marks)*

|  |  | sperm Dd | |
|---|---|---|---|
|  |  | D | d |
| eggs dd | d | Dd | dd |
|  | d | Dd | dd |

### EXAM ALERT!

Practise completing Punnett squares to clearly show your prediction of the outcome of a given cross.

Students have struggled with exam questions similar to this – **be prepared!**

## Now try this

**1** (target G-E) Which **one** of these disorders is caused by a single gene: measles, polydactyly, diabetes? *(1 mark)*

**2** (target D-C) Look at the polydactyly Punnett square in the Worked Example. What is the possible chance of inheriting polydactyly from a parent who has one allele for the disorder? *(1 mark)*

Had a look ☐   Nearly there ☐   Nailed it! ☐

**BIOLOGY 2.7.3**

# Family trees

CYSTIC FIBROSIS is an inherited disorder that affects cell membranes, and makes mucus stickier than normal.

Cystic fibrosis is caused by having two copies of a recessive allele.

If we use F for the dominant allele that doesn't cause cystic fibrosis, and f for the recessive allele:

- a person who is FF will not have the disorder and cannot pass it on to offspring
- a person who is ff has cystic fibrosis
- a person who is Ff does not have the disorder but can pass on the disorder to their children – we say they are CARRIERS.

This Punnett diagram shows that two parents who are carriers for cystic fibrosis have a 1 in 4 chance of having a child with the disorder.

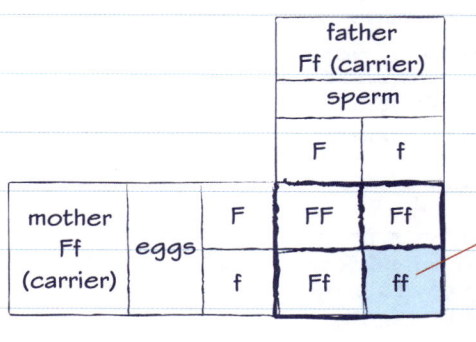

|  |  | father Ff (carrier) | |
|---|---|---|---|
|  |  | sperm | |
|  |  | F | f |
| mother Ff (carrier) | eggs F | FF | Ff |
|  | f | Ff | ff |

A child with these alleles will develop cystic fibrosis.

---

This FAMILY TREE shows the inheritance of cystic fibrosis in one family. It shows which members of the family have the disorder and which do not. Knowing how cystic fibrosis can be inherited, we can work out which family members may be carriers for the disorder.

Three generations are shown in this pedigree. Arun and Beth are the oldest generation.

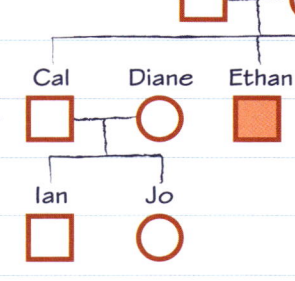

Generation 1: Arun — Beth
Generation 2: Cal — Diane, Ethan, Gill — Harry
Generation 3: Ian, Jo (children of Cal and Diane); Laurie, Mia (children of Gill and Harry)

Ethan has cystic fibrosis. Mia has cystic fibrosis.

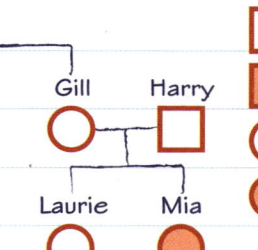

KEY
☐ male, no cystic fibrosis
■ male, cystic fibrosis
○ female, no cystic fibrosis
● female, cystic fibrosis

---

## Worked example (target D–C)

**Explain** (AQA SKILL, Page 101)

Look at the family tree above. Explain why Arun and Beth must both be carriers of cystic fibrosis. *(2 marks)*

Ethan has cystic fibrosis so he must have inherited one allele for the disorder from Arun and one from Beth. Neither Arun nor Beth have the disorder, so they must have one cystic fibrosis allele and one allele that doesn't cause cystic fibrosis, and so they are carriers.

## Now try this

**1** (target G–E) Look at the family tree above. Ethan has cystic fibrosis. Name **one** other family member who has cystic fibrosis. *(1 mark)*

**2** (target D–C)
(a) In the family tree above, identify **two** people, other than Arun and Beth, who are carriers for cystic fibrosis. *(1 mark)*
(b) Explain your answer to part (a). *(2 marks)*

# Embryo screening

People who have, or think they have, an allele for an inherited disorder can decide to have their embryo screened at a very early stage of a pregnancy.

EMBRYO SCREENING tests the embryo for specific alleles. If it is certain that the embryo will develop an inherited disorder, the couple can ask a doctor to terminate the pregnancy (have an abortion).

## Issues with embryo screening

There are many issues with embryo screening. Different people will have different answers to these questions, depending on their point of view.

**ECONOMIC ISSUES:** related to money
- Will it cost parents extra money to support a child with the disorder?
- Does someone with the disorder need lots of hospital treatment or drugs?

**SOCIAL ISSUES:** related to people and society
- If the child needs care throughout life, who will do it if the parents cannot?
- If the child needs lots of care, is this fair on other children in the family?

**ETHICAL ISSUES:** related to right and wrong, or fairness
- Does an embryo have the same right to life as a person? if so, is it right to abort an embryo that will develop the disease?
- Screening carries a very small risk of damaging the embryo – should parents take the risk?

### Worked example

Sickle cell disease is an inherited disorder that is caused by a recessive allele. Sickle cell disease can cause a lot of pain and can shorten life. Couples who have close relatives with sickle cell disease may be offered embryo screening. Give **one** reason why some people support embryo screening and one reason why some people are against embryo screening. *(2 marks)*

Some people support embryo screening because it gives parents the chance to terminate the pregnancy if the embryo will develop an inherited disease. This will avoid suffering for the child and for the parents. Some people are against embryo screening because they are against the idea of terminating any pregnancy.

You may be given an unfamiliar example of an inherited disorder in a question about embryo screening. Use what you know about the issues of embryo screening to answer the question.

### EXAM ALERT!

Different answers than the one given above could also be marked correct as long as they are well supported by reasons.

Students have struggled with exam questions similar to this – **be prepared!**

### Now try this

1. Complete the sentence. Embryo _____ can test for alleles that cause _____ disorders. *(2 marks)*

2. A couple know that they are both carriers of the allele that causes cystic fibrosis. Neither of them have the disorder. Explain why they might choose to have their embryos screened for the disorder. *(2 marks)*

Had a look ☐    Nearly there ☐    Nailed it! ☐    **BIOLOGY 2.8.1**

# Fossils

Evidence for early forms of life comes from fossils. FOSSILS are the 'remains' of organisms from many years ago and are found in rocks.

## Fossil formation

Fossils are formed in various ways.

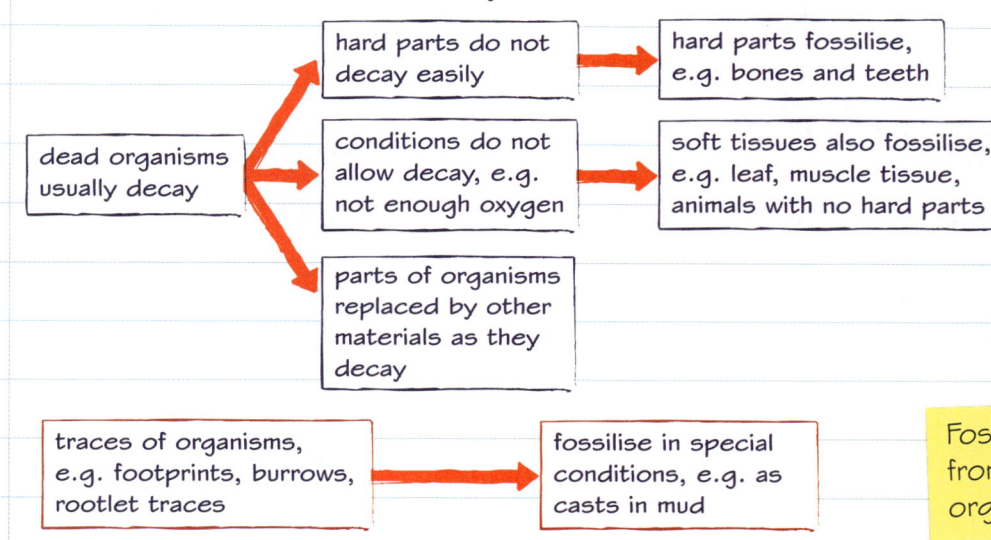

- dead organisms usually decay
  - hard parts do not decay easily → hard parts fossilise, e.g. bones and teeth
  - conditions do not allow decay, e.g. not enough oxygen → soft tissues also fossilise, e.g. leaf, muscle tissue, animals with no hard parts
  - parts of organisms replaced by other materials as they decay

- traces of organisms, e.g. footprints, burrows, rootlet traces → fossilise in special conditions, e.g. as casts in mud

Fossils like this are formed from the hard parts of a dead organism such as bones.

## Fossil evidence

The age of a fossil can be worked out from the rock it is in.

This can show how much or how little organisms have changed over millions of years.

## Loss of fossil evidence

The fossil record is not complete because:
- fossils only form in special conditions
- many early life forms had soft bodies that left few traces
- geological changes in rocks over time destroy some fossils.

### Worked example (target D-C)

**AQA SKILL: Suggest** (Page 101)

The first signs of organisms on Earth are of bacteria in rocks 3.8 billion years old. Scientists are not certain if they evolved from simple chemicals on Earth or if they arrived on meteorites from other parts of the Solar System. Suggest **two** reasons why scientists cannot be certain how life began on Earth. *(2 marks)*

Bacteria are very small and so don't fossilise easily. Geological changes over billions of years have destroyed a lot of the evidence of fossil bacteria in those rocks. So there is not enough evidence to be sure.

### Now try this

1. (target G-E) What is meant by a **fossil**? *(1 mark)*

2. (target D-C) Give **one** reason why:
   (a) we have more evidence of how vertebrates (animals with bones) have evolved than of soft-bodied animals *(1 mark)*
   (b) we do not have a continuous record of fossils showing the evolution of any animal or plant. *(1 mark)*

**BIOLOGY 2.8.1**  Had a look ☐   Nearly there ☐   Nailed it! ☐

# Extinction

EXTINCTION is when all individuals of a species die out.

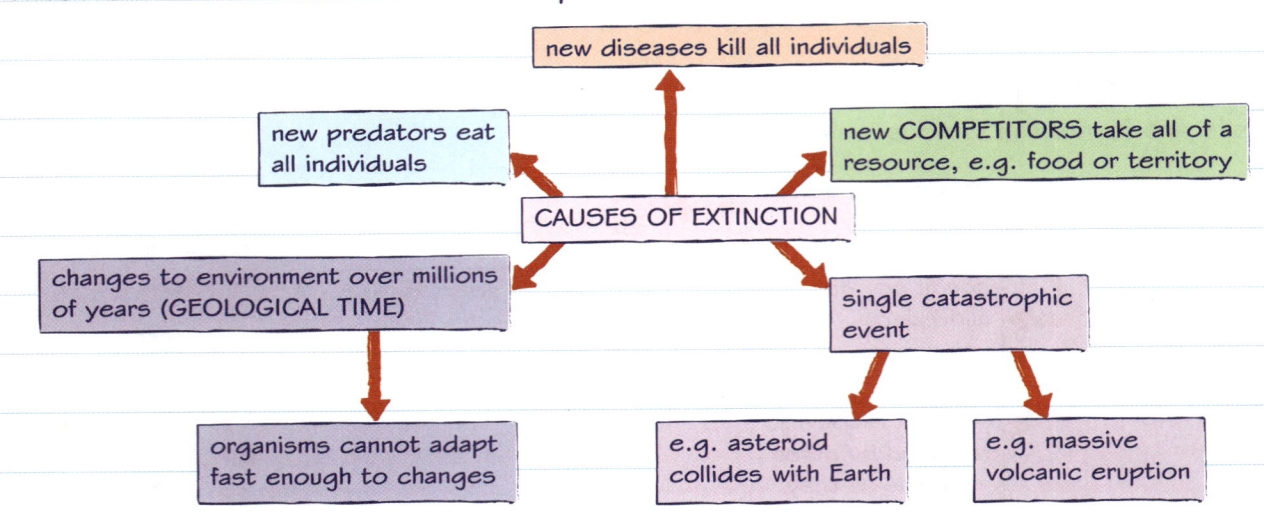

**Causes of extinction:**
- new diseases kill all individuals
- new predators eat all individuals
- new COMPETITORS take all of a resource, e.g. food or territory
- changes to environment over millions of years (GEOLOGICAL TIME) → organisms cannot adapt fast enough to changes
- single catastrophic event → e.g. asteroid collides with Earth; e.g. massive volcanic eruption

Sometimes a species 'disappears' from the fossil record because it has changed so much that it is given a different species name.

You may be given an example of extinction in a question. Use information in the diagram above to help you answer the question.

## Worked example (target D-C)

Anole lizards live on islands in the Caribbean. Each island has its own species, although DNA evidence suggests that some species are very closely related. The lizards cannot move between the islands. Suggest how these species arose. *(2 marks)*

Individuals were separated by water between the islands. The lizards on each island evolved into a new species.

## Now try this

**1** (target G-E) Choose the correct ending below to complete this sentence:

Dinosaurs became extinct 65 million years ago, which means that …

A … they were all killed by an asteroid hitting Earth.

B … there is no sign of living dinosaurs on Earth since 65 million years ago.

C … we might be able to create new dinosaurs from DNA. *(1 mark)*

**2** (target D-C) Hawaii is an island 2300 miles from the mainland. Evidence shows that humans landed on Hawaii about 1000 years ago, bringing rats with them. Soon after that, many Hawaiian species became extinct. Suggest **two** possible reasons for the extinctions. *(2 marks)*

Had a look ☐   Nearly there ☐   Nailed it! ☐   **BIOLOGY**

# Biology six mark question 3

There will be one 6 mark question on your exam paper, which will be marked for *quality of written communication* as well as scientific knowledge. This means that you need to apply your scientific knowledge, present your answer in a logical and organised way, and make sure that your spelling, grammar and punctuation are as good as you can make them.

## Worked example

The diagram shows two generations of a family tree for an inherited disorder called sickle cell disorder. This disorder is caused by a recessive allele.

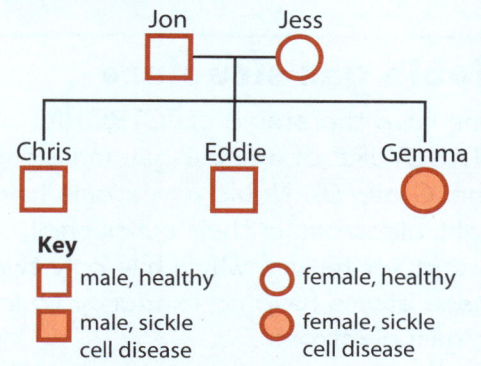

```
        Jon ─── Jess
         □       ○
         │
    ┌────┼────┐
  Chris Eddie Gemma
    □    □    ●
```

**Key**
☐ male, healthy   ○ female, healthy
■ male, sickle cell disease   ● female, sickle cell disease

Use the family tree to help you explain as fully as possible why Gemma has the disorder but her two brothers do not. *(6 marks)*

As the disorder is caused by a recessive allele, this means you have to have two of the alleles to get the disorder. So Gemma must have two alleles for sickle cell disorder. Her brothers don't have the disorder, so they must either have two healthy alleles that don't cause sickle cell disease or one healthy allele and one sickle cell allele.

Gemma inherited her alleles from her parents, Jon and Jess. Chris and Eddie also got their alleles from Jon and Jess, so Jon and Jess must be carriers of the sickle cell allele.

### Using information
Often questions will contain information. In this case it is the family tree. Make sure you use this information when answering the question.

This part of the answer could have been answered using letters for the alleles. For example if N stands for the dominant non-sickle cell/healthy allele, and n for the recessive sickle cell allele, then Gemma must be nn, while her brothers could be Nn or NN.

This would be even better if it said that each child inherits one allele from each parent when their gametes fuse during fertilisation. So each child inherits one of their two alleles for this gene from each parent. Jon and Jess must both have one healthy allele and one sickle cell allele, which makes them carriers for the disorder.

## Now try this

The oldest known fossils of multicelled organisms are found in rocks that are over 540 million years old. The fossils show these organisms had soft bodies. In younger rocks, fossils of completely different organisms are found. Suggest how the oldest fossils were formed and give reasons why they have disappeared from the fossil record. *(6 marks)*

# Forming ions

An ION forms when an atom loses or gains one or more electrons.

## Positive ions

Metal atoms and hydrogen atoms lose electrons to form positive ions.

For example, a sodium atom loses its outer electron to form a sodium ion, $Na^+$.

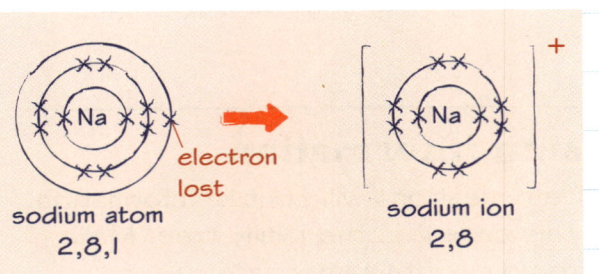

sodium atom 2,8,1 → sodium ion 2,8 (electron lost)

## Negative ions

Non-metal atoms gain electrons to form negative ions.

For example, a chlorine atom gains one outer electron to form a chloride ion, $Cl^-$.

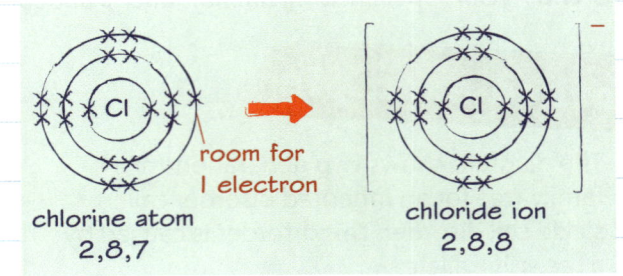

chlorine atom 2,8,7 → chloride ion 2,8,8 (room for 1 electron)

## Patterns in the Periodic Table

Remember:
- The number of charges on a positive ion is the same as the group number of the element.
- The number of charges on a negative ion is 8 minus the group number of the element.

| Group | 1 | 2 | 3 | 5 | 6 | 7 |
|---|---|---|---|---|---|---|
| Charge on ion | + | 2+ | 3+ | 3− | 2− | − |

## Noble gas structure

Ions have the stable ELECTRONIC STRUCTURE of a noble gas (an element from Group 0). Noble gas atoms have eight electrons in their outer shell, except for helium, which has only two. These atoms have no tendency to lose or gain electrons.

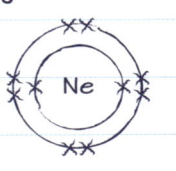

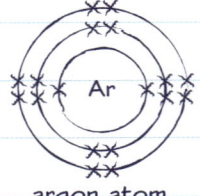

neon atom 2,8    argon atom 2,8,8

### Worked example (target D-C)

(a) Complete the diagram to show the electronic structure of a fluoride ion. *(1 mark)*

(b) What is the electronic structure of a fluoride ion? *(1 mark)*

2,8

The nucleus stays the same when an ion forms, so the atom does not actually turn into a noble gas.

Remember that the outer shell is always full in an ion.

## Now try this

**target G-E**

1. (a) How does a bromine atom become a bromide ion, $Br^-$? *(1 mark)*
   (b) How does a magnesium atom become a magnesium ion, $Mg^{2+}$? *(1 mark)*

2. The first diagram shows the electronic structure of an oxygen atom. Complete the second diagram to show the electronic structure of an oxide ion. *(1 mark)*

**target D-C**

3. Nitrogen is in Group 5, and can form nitride ions. Give the charge on a nitride ion and explain your answer. *(2 marks)*

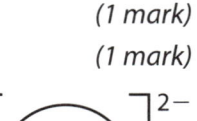

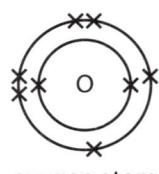

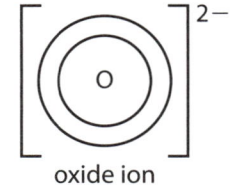

Had a look ☐ Nearly there ☐ Nailed it! ☐  CHEMISTRY 2.1.1

# Ionic compounds

Ionic compounds contain positive and negative ions, formed when atoms transfer electrons.

## Group 1 elements (the alkali metals)

The elements in Group 1:
- are metals
- react with non-metal elements to form ionic compounds
- produce ions with a 1+ charge.

Lithium, sodium and potassium are in Group 1.

## Group 7 elements (the halogens)

The elements in Group 7:
- are non-metals
- react with metal elements to form ionic compounds
- produce ions with a 1− charge.

Chlorine, bromine and iodine are in Group 7.

## Forming ionic compounds

Group 1 elements react with Group 7 elements to produce ionic compounds. For example, sodium reacts with chlorine to form sodium chloride. This contains sodium ions, $Na^+$, and chloride ions, $Cl^-$.

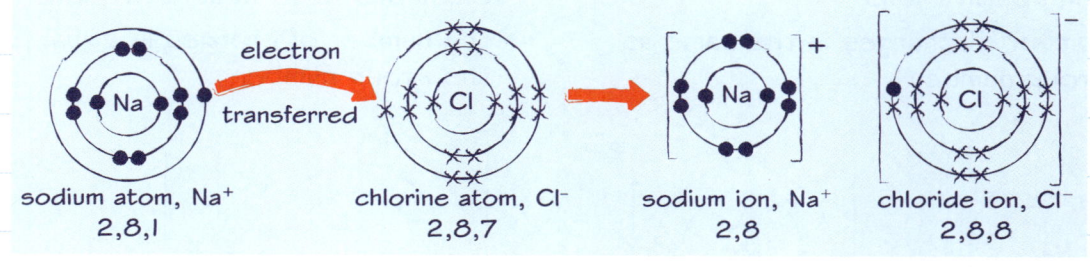

sodium atom, $Na^+$ — 2,8,1 → electron transferred → chlorine atom, $Cl^-$ — 2,8,7 → sodium ion, $Na^+$ — 2,8 | chloride ion, $Cl^-$ — 2,8,8

The electron from the highest occupied energy level of a sodium atom is transferred to the highest occupied energy level of a chlorine atom, forming an $Na^+$ ion and a $Cl^-$ ion.

## Worked example — target D-C

Give the formulae of the following compounds.

(a) sodium chloride (1 mark)
NaCl

(b) calcium chloride (1 mark)
$CaCl_2$

(c) magnesium oxide (1 mark)
MgO

Use the table on page 98 to work out the charge on each ion. The number of positive and negative charges in the compound must be the same.

$Na^+$ and $Cl^-$ gives NaCl.

$Ca^{2+}$ and two $Cl^-$ gives $CaCl_2$.

$Mg^{2+}$ and $O^{2-}$ gives MgO.

## Now try this

**1** Copper(II) chloride, $CuCl_2$, is an ionic compound. (target G-E)
  (a) What are the names of the ions in the compound? (1 mark)
  (b) How many negative ions are in the formula for copper(II) chloride? (1 mark)

**2** Magnesium chloride is an ionic compound that contains magnesium ions ($Mg^{2+}$) and chloride ions ($Cl^-$). (target D-C)
  (a) Draw a diagram to show the electronic structure of a chloride ion. (2 marks)
  (b) Explain how a chlorine atom changes into a chloride ion. (1 mark)
  (c) Give the formula of magnesium chloride. (1 mark)

**3** Give the formula of sodium oxide. (1 mark)

# CHEMISTRY 2.1.1

Had a look ☐    Nearly there ☐    Nailed it! ☐

# Giant ionic structures

## Ionic bonds

An ionic compound is a GIANT STRUCTURE of ions. The ions are held in a regular arrangement called a lattice.

IONIC BONDS are strong electrostatic forces of attraction between oppositely charged ions. They act in all directions in the ionic lattice, holding the structure together.

## Representing the lattice

This diagram shows the arrangement of ions in an ionic compound such as sodium chloride, NaCl.

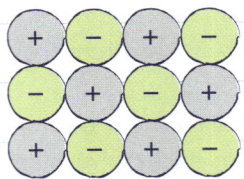

## Representing positive ions

Remember:
- metal atoms lose one or more electrons to form positive ions
- the number of charges is the same as the group number.

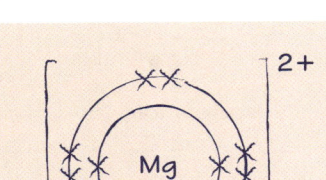

## Representing negative ions

Remember:
- non-metal atoms gain one or more electrons to form negative ions
- the number of charges is equal to 8 minus the group number.

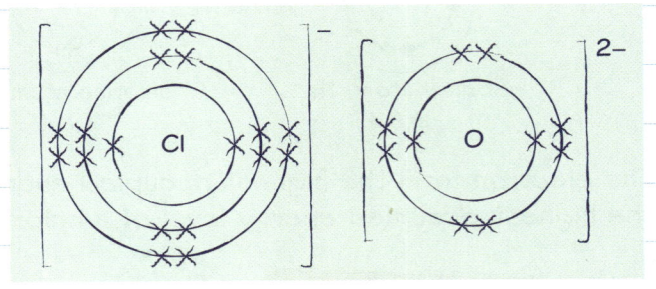

## Worked example (target D-C)

**AQA SKILL: Draw — Page 101**

Draw the electronic structure of a calcium ion, $Ca^{2+}$. (1 mark)

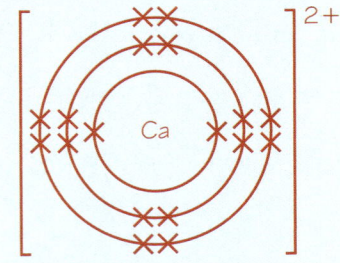

You need to be able to represent the ions in sodium chloride, magnesium oxide and calcium chloride. This means $Na^+$, $Mg^{2+}$, $Ca^{2+}$, $Cl^-$ and $O^{2-}$ ions.

You may be given a diagram showing the shells, or a diagram to show you the required style. You then need to add the electrons.

## Now try this (target D-C)

1. Explain why the ions stay in place in the sodium chloride lattice. (2 marks)
2. Describe an ionic bond. (2 marks)
3. (a) Draw a diagram to show the electronic structure of an oxide ion. (2 marks)
   (b) Draw a diagram to show the electronic structure of a magnesium ion. (2 marks)
   (c) Explain why these two ions have the same electronic structure but a different charge. (2 marks)

Had a look ☐   Nearly there ☐   Nailed it! ☐

**CHEMISTRY 2.1.4**

# Covalent bonds in simple molecules

COVALENT BONDS form when atoms share electrons.

## Covalent bonds

A covalent bond is a shared pair of electrons. It forms between two non-metal atoms.

Covalent bonds are strong.

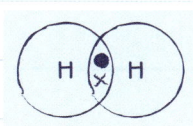

> The number of covalent bonds an atom can form is usually 8 minus its group number.

## Representing covalent bonds

A covalent bond can be shown in two other ways:

H–H (where the straight line is the bond), and

H •ₓ H

This diagram is like the one on the left, but without the circle that shows the highest occupied energy level (outer shell).

> The shared electron from one atom is shown as a dot, and the other electron as a cross. But the electrons are actually no different.

## Representing simple molecules

Hydrogen exists as simple molecules. A simple molecule contains only a few atoms joined together by covalent bonds. The diagrams show the bonding in other simple molecules.

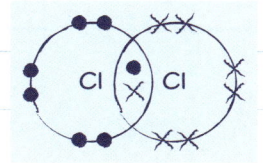

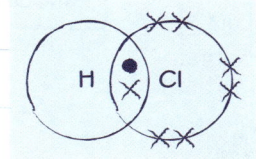

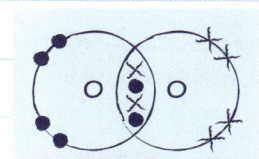

> The two oxygen atoms in an oxygen molecule are joined by a double covalent bond. This is two shared pairs of electrons, shown as O=O. You only need to show the outer shells in these diagrams.

### Worked example — target G-E

Draw a diagram to the show the bonding in ammonia, $NH_3$. Use a straight line for each bond. *(1 mark)*

H—N—H
     |
     H

### Worked example — target D-C

Complete this dot and cross diagram to show the bonding in water. *(2 marks)*

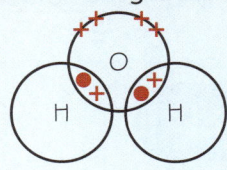

## Now try this

1  What is a covalent bond?  *(1 mark)*  — target G-E

2  Draw a dot and cross diagram to show the bonding in methane, $CH_4$.  *(3 marks)*  — target D-C

# CHEMISTRY 2.1.1

Had a look ☐   Nearly there ☐   Nailed it! ☐

# Covalent bonds in macromolecules

## Macromolecules

MACROMOLECULES have a giant covalent structure. Each molecule contains very many atoms joined together by covalent bonds.

Macromolecules can be:
- elements, like diamond (a form of carbon)
- compounds, like silica (silicon dioxide).

> The covalent bonds in macromolecules are usually represented by straight lines, rather than dots and crosses.

## Diamond

A diamond is a single molecule containing carbon atoms. Each carbon atom is covalently bonded to four other carbon atoms, forming a giant covalent structure.

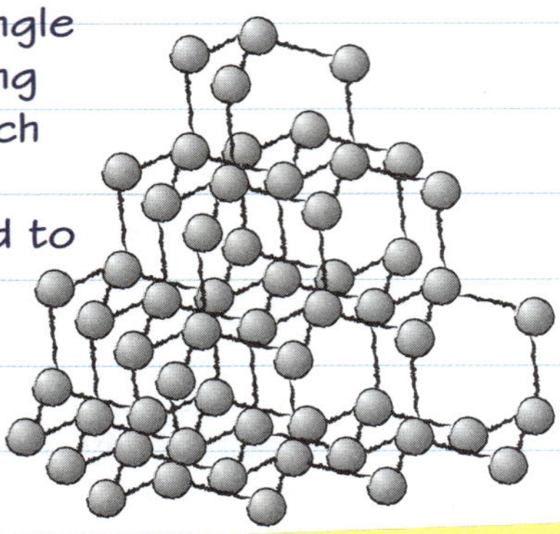

> Diamond and silica have similar structures, even though they contain different atoms.

## Silica

Sand contains silica. Each silicon atom is covalently bonded to four oxygen atoms, and each oxygen atom is covalently bonded to two silicon atoms. This gives it the formula $SiO_2$, which is why it is also called silicon dioxide.

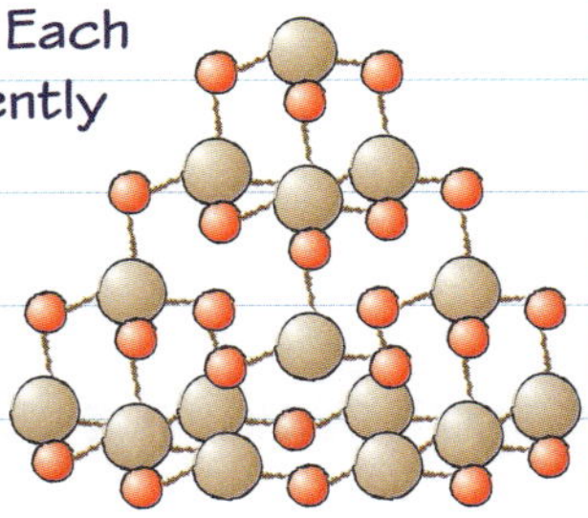

## Worked example (target D-C)

The diagram shows the outer electron shells for five carbon atoms in diamond.

Draw the positions of all the electrons in the outer shells of all five atoms. *(3 marks)*

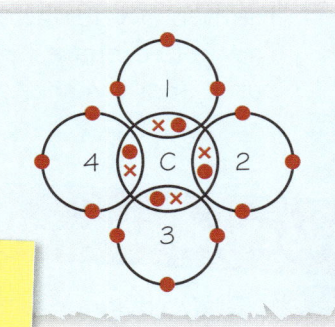

> Atoms 1, 2, 3 and 4 will each be bonded to three other carbon atoms, not just the middle one. There would be no need to try to draw these other carbon atoms as well.

## Now try this (target G-E)

1. What type of bonding is present in simple molecules and macromolecules? *(1 mark)*

2. The diagrams show two molecules, A and B. Explain which one represents a macromolecule. *(2 marks)*

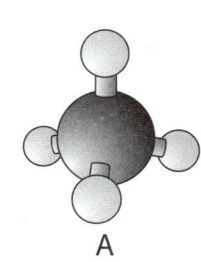

A 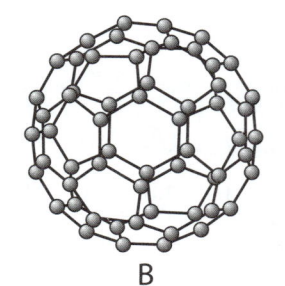       B

Had a look ☐  Nearly there ☐  Nailed it! ☐    **CHEMISTRY 2.2.1 & 2.2.2**

# Properties of molecules

Simple molecules and macromolecules both contain covalent bonds, but they have different properties.

## Simple molecules

Simple molecules such as $O_2$ and $H_2O$ have:
- relatively low melting points
- relatively low boiling points.

They tend to be gases or liquids at room temperature, but can be solids (such as wax).

The molecules have no overall electrical charge, so they do not conduct electricity.

## Macromolecules

Macromolecules such as silica, diamond and graphite have:
- very high melting points.

Their atoms are joined by strong covalent bonds to form a network of atoms called a giant covalent lattice.

## Diamond

The carbon atoms in diamond form a lattice.

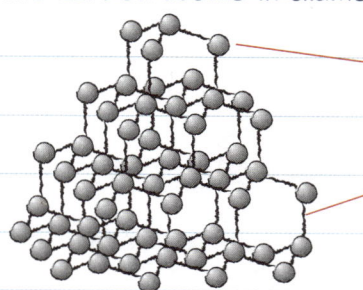

- Each atom is bonded to four others.
- Strong covalent bonds between atoms.

## Graphite

The carbon atoms in graphite form layers.

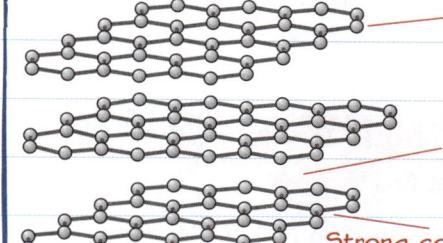

- Each atom is bonded to three others.
- No covalent bonds between the layers.
- Strong covalent bonds between atoms in a layer.

### Worked example  (target D-C)

**Explain why diamond is used for cutting tools but graphite is used for pencils.** (4 marks)

Diamond is hard because each atom is joined to four other carbon atoms by covalent bonds. Graphite is soft and slippery because it has no covalent bonds between its layers, so the layers can slide over each other easily.

Diamond and graphite both contain carbon atoms joined by covalent bonds, but graphite has a layered structure. The difference in structure explains their different properties. Diamond is hard enough to be used for tile cutters and drill bits. Graphite can be used as a lubricant.

### Now try this

1. Draw a ring around the correct answer to complete each sentence. (target G-E)
   (a) Diamond has a high melting point because **several / all / few** atoms are joined by strong bonds. (1 mark)
   (b) Each atom in diamond is joined to **two / three / four** other atoms. (1 mark)

2. The diagram shows the structure of graphene. It is made of carbon atoms and is similar to a single layer of graphite. (target D-C)
   (a) How many atoms is each atom in graphene joined to? (1 mark)
   (b) Name the type of bond between the atoms in graphene. (1 mark)

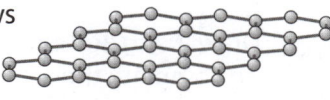

37

# CHEMISTRY 2.2.3

Had a look ☐   Nearly there ☐   Nailed it! ☐

# Properties of ionic compounds

The properties of ionic compounds, such as sodium chloride and magnesium oxide, can be explained by their structure and bonding.

## Melting and boiling points

The diagram shows part of the ionic lattice of a crystal of sodium chloride.

Ionic compounds like sodium chloride have:
- high melting points
- high boiling points.

— $Na^+$ ion
— $Cl^-$ ion

Large amounts of energy are needed to break the many strong ionic bonds in ionic compounds. This is why ionic compounds are solid at room temperature.

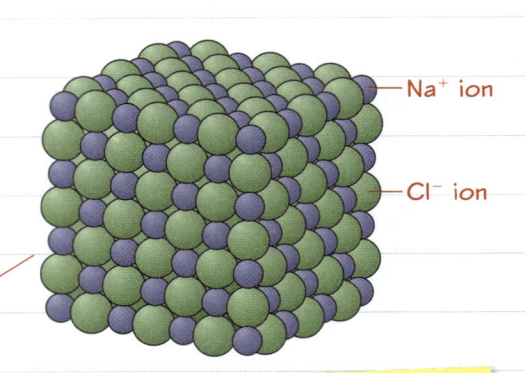

An **ionic bond** is an electrostatic force of attraction between oppositely charged ions.

## Worked example (target D-C)

Sodium sulfate contains $Na^+$ ions and $SO_4^{2-}$ ions.

**(a)** Write the formula for sodium sulfate. *(1 mark)*

$Na_2SO_4$

**(b)** Why does sodium sulfate **not** conduct electricity when solid? *(1 mark)*

The ions are not free to move around in a solid.

**(c)** Explain **one** way to make sodium sulfate conduct electricity. *(2 marks)*

Dissolve it in water. The ions will then be free to move around and carry the current.

## EXAM ALERT!

Remember that you should be able to write formulae for ionic compounds from given symbols for ions.

Students have struggled with exam questions similar to this – **be prepared!**

Ions are charged but they cannot carry an electric current if they cannot move about.

Ions are also free to move around and carry the current when an ionic substance is molten (melted to form a liquid). As ionic substances have high melting points, it is often better to try to dissolve them so that they conduct electricity. This will not be possible if the ionic compound is insoluble in water.

## Now try this

**1** (target G-E) Draw a ring around the correct answer to complete the sentence.

Sodium chloride has a high melting point because it has many

| strong ionic | strong covalent | weak ionic |

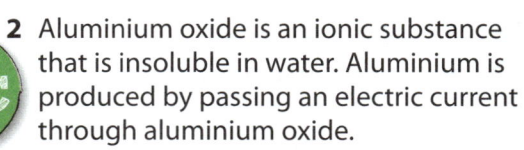

bonds. *(1 mark)*

**2** (target D-C) Aluminium oxide is an ionic substance that is insoluble in water. Aluminium is produced by passing an electric current through aluminium oxide.

**(a)** Explain how to make aluminium oxide conduct electricity. *(2 marks)*

**(b)** Suggest why doing what you suggest in part **(a)** might be expensive. *(2 marks)*

Had a look ☐   Nearly there ☐   Nailed it! ☐   **CHEMISTRY 2.2.4**

# Metals

## Giant structures of atoms

Metals consist of giant structures of atoms, arranged in a regular pattern. Their properties can be explained by this structure. For example, metals can be bent and shaped because the layers of atoms can slide over each other.

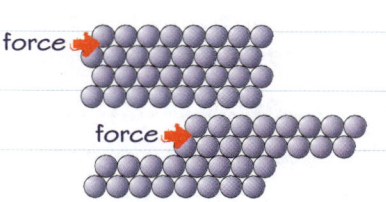

---

### Worked example (D-C)

Pure copper contains layers of copper atoms. Copper is mixed with zinc to make brass.

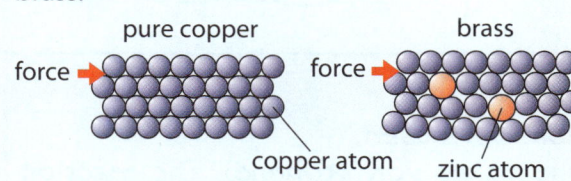

*pure copper* — *brass* (with copper atom and zinc atom labelled)

Suggest why brass is harder than copper. *(2 marks)*

The larger zinc atoms disrupt the layers. This means that the copper atoms cannot slide over each other so easily.

An **alloy** is a metal mixed with one or more other elements, usually other metals. Alloys are usually harder than the pure metals alone. **Shape memory alloys** can return to their original shape after being stretched or bent. Nitinol is one of these alloys. It is used in dental braces.

---

### Worked example (D-C)

Solder is a metal that is used to join electrical components. It must be melted so it can be applied. One solder is an alloy of tin and lead. Use the data in the table to answer the question.

| Metal | How well it conducts electricity | Melting point in °C |
|---|---|---|
| tin | 1.8 | 232 |
| lead | 1.0 | 327 |
| solder | 1.4 | 183 |

Explain why solder is a better choice for joining delicate electrical components than tin or lead on their own. *(3 marks)*

Although solder is the second best of the three metals at conducting electricity, it has the lowest melting point. This means that it is less likely to damage the electrical components when the liquid solder is used to join components.

Notice that solder, the alloy of tin and lead, has different properties from the metals it is made from.

---

### Now try this

**1** (target G-E)
(a) What is an **alloy**? *(1 mark)*
(b) Describe how the atoms are arranged in a metal. *(2 marks)*

**2** (target D-C) The table shows some information about iron and some types of steel (alloys of iron and carbon).

| % carbon | 0 | 0.2 | 0.4 | 0.8 |
|---|---|---|---|---|
| Relative strength | 1.0 | 1.8 | 2.6 | 3.3 |
| How well it resists cracking | 2.9 | 2.1 | 1.6 | 1.0 |

(a) Suggest **one** advantage and **one** disadvantage of using steels containing 1.2% carbon. *(2 marks)*
(b) Explain why adding carbon to iron changes the strength of the metal. *(3 marks)*

**CHEMISTRY 2.2.5** — Had a look ☐  Nearly there ☐  Nailed it! ☐

# Polymers

Polymers are very large molecules made when small molecules (monomers) join together. There are different types of polymers with different uses.

## Thermosoftening polymers

Thermosoftening polymers consist of individual, tangled polymer chains.

Thermosoftening polymers:
- soften and melt when heated
- include poly(ethene) and poly(propene).

*tangled but no cross-links*

## Thermosetting polymers

Thermosetting polymers consist of polymer chains with cross-links between them.

*cross-links*

### LDPE and HDPE

The properties of polymers depend upon the monomers used.

Ethene is used to make poly(ethene) and propene makes poly(propene). The reaction conditions are also important. There are two forms of poly(ethene) depending on the reaction conditions used:
- LDPE – low-density poly(ethene)
- HDPE – high-density poly(ethene).

For example, LDPE is made at a different temperature and pressures than HDPE. Different catalysts are also used.

LDPE and HDPE have different uses because they have different properties.

## Worked example (target D-C)

**AQA SKILL: Explain** (Page 101)

The table shows properties of LDPE and HDPE. A plastic becomes too soft to use above its highest useful temperature.

| Property | LDPE | HDPE |
|---|---|---|
| Highest useful temperature in °C | 80 | 110 |
| Relative strength | low | high |
| Flexibility | high | low |

Explain which polymer would be best for making plastic drinks cups. *(3 marks)*

HDPE would be best. It is stronger and less flexible than LDPE, which would make a cup easier to hold. Its highest useful temperature is above the boiling point of water, so the cup could hold hot drinks.

### EXAM ALERT!

You may be given data in the exam about unfamiliar polymers so that you can explain the uses of the polymers.

Students have struggled with exam questions similar to this – **be prepared!**

## Now try this

**target G-E**

1. What happens when a thermosoftening polymer is heated? *(1 mark)*

2. How can you tell from a diagram that a polymer is a thermosetting polymer? *(1 mark)*

**target D-C**

3. Use the table in the worked example to explain which polymer (LDPE or HDPE) would be best for making a supermarket carrier bag. *(3 marks)*

Had a look ☐   Nearly there ☐   Nailed it! ☐   **CHEMISTRY 2.2.6**

# Nanoscience

NANOSCIENCE concerns structures between 1 nm and 100 nm in size.

NANOPARTICLES may each contain only a few hundred atoms. Their small size means that they have:
- a high surface area to volume ratio
- properties different from the same substance in larger pieces.

*1 nm is one nanometre. It is one millionth of a millimetre.*

## Uses of nanoparticles

The special properties of nanoparticles may lead to the development of new:
- ✓ computers
- ✓ catalysts
- ✓ coatings, for example on self-cleaning windows
- ✓ highly selective sensors to detect substances such as polluting gases
- ✓ lighter and stronger construction materials
- ✓ cosmetics such as sunscreens and deodorants.

### Nanotubes

Nanotubes are one example of nanoparticles. They are made of carbon and have a structure similar to a graphite layer rolled into a tube.

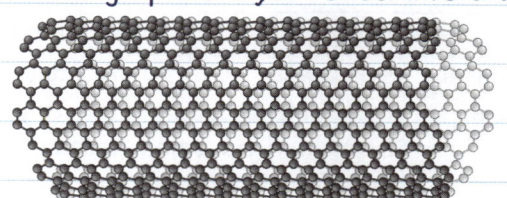

Nanotubes:
- are very strong
- conduct electricity.

They are used to strengthen tennis rackets and golf clubs. They may lead to the development of new, faster computers.

## Worked example  target D-C

**AQA SKILL: Suggest, Page 101**

Buckyballs are nanoparticles that can absorb large amounts of hydrogen. Hydrogen is a gas at room temperature. It could be used as a fuel for cars and releases only water when it burns.

Suggest why car manufacturers may be interested in nanoscience research. *(2 marks)*

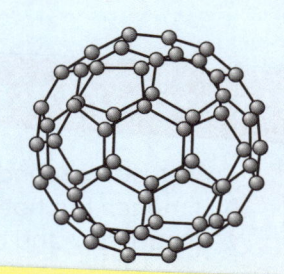

*If buckyballs can absorb large amounts of hydrogen, they could be used to store hydrogen for cars. This would let car manufacturers make cars that run on a 'clean' fuel.*

*Nanotubes and buckyballs are examples of **fullerenes**.*

## Now try this

**target G-E**
1. Draw a ring around the correct answer to complete the sentence.
   Nanoparticles contain a few | million atoms  thousand atoms  hundred atoms |. *(1 mark)*

**target D-C**
2. Vanadium dioxide is a blue powder. Scientists have developed a product that contains vanadium dioxide nanoparticles. These nanoparticles are invisible when they are applied to glass, but they significantly reduce the amount of heat energy transferred through the glass.

   (a) Explain why vanadium dioxide is blue but the coating is invisible. *(2 marks)*

   (b) Suggest **two** advantages of using this new coating when putting windows into a new building. *(2 marks)*

# CHEMISTRY 2.2.3

Had a look ☐   Nearly there ☐   Nailed it! ☐

# Different structures

The properties of a substance give clues about its type of structure.

| Structure | Simple molecular | Macromolecular (giant covalent) | Ionic | Metallic |
|---|---|---|---|---|
| Examples | $O_2$, $H_2$, $H_2O$, $CH_4$ | diamond, silica, graphite | NaCl, MgO, $CaCl_2$ | metals |
| Bonding | covalent | covalent | ionic | metallic |
| Arrangement of particles | separate molecules, each containing a small number of atoms joined together | giant structure of very many atoms joined together | giant ionic lattice in which oppositely charged ions are attracted to each other | giant structure of atoms arranged in a regular pattern |
| Melting and boiling points | low | very high | high | high |
| Do they conduct electricity? | ✗ | ✗ diamond and silica ✓ graphite | ✗ when solid ✓ when dissolved in water or melted | ✓ |
| Can be bent when solid? | ✗ | ✗ | ✗ | ✓ |

## Worked example (target D-C)

**AQA SPEC SKILL**

A substance conducts electricity when it is molten but not when it is solid. Describe its structure and bonding. *(2 marks)*

It consists of a giant ionic lattice containing oppositely charged ions. These are attracted to each other by ionic bonds.

> A metal would conduct electricity when it is solid as well as when it is a liquid.

> Ionic bonds are strong electrostatic forces of attraction between charged particles (ions) that act in all directions.

## Now try this

**1** (target G-E) Draw a ring around the correct answer to complete the sentence.

Petrol is a liquid at room temperature. Its type of structure is

| ionic    simple molecular |
| giant molecular |

*(1 mark)*

**2** (target D-C) A substance is solid at room temperature. It conducts electricity but breaks when you try to bend it.

(a) What type of structure does this substance have? *(1 mark)*

(b) Suggest what this substance might be. *(1 mark)*

Had a look ☐  Nearly there ☐  Nailed it! ☐   **CHEMISTRY**

# Chemistry six mark question 1

There will be one 6 mark question on your exam paper, which will be marked for *quality of written communication* as well as scientific knowledge. This means that you need to apply your scientific knowledge, present your answer in a logical and organised way, and make sure that your spelling, grammar and punctuation are as good as you can make them.

## Worked example

Silver can kill bacteria. Silver nanoparticles are used in some socks, plasters, kitchen chopping boards and washing machines.

However, some people are allergic to silver. If swallowed in large amounts, silver nitrate causes vomiting, diarrhoea and even death. Normal-sized particles are safe on the skin, but nanoparticles might pass into the body.

Explain why nanoparticles may have different properties than ordinary silver. Describe advantages and disadvantages of adding silver nanoparticles to products. *(6 marks)*

Nanoparticles are only 1–100 nm in size, so they may be small enough to pass through skin and into the blood. They have a much higher surface area than the same amount of ordinary silver, giving them different properties.

Silver is expensive, so nanoparticles mean that the metal can be used more cheaply. They kill bacteria, which may prevent illness and keep clothes fresh for longer. However, silver might cause allergic reactions, and the nanoparticles might cause illness or death if they pass into the body.

### Using information

The information given will help you with your answer, but you should not just repeat it.

Use your scientific knowledge to explain the properties of silver nanoparticles, and the information given to describe detailed advantages and disadvantages of using them. Make sure you give both advantages and disadvantages.

> The answer gives two reasons why nanoparticles may have different properties from ordinary silver, including how they might get into the body without being swallowed.

> The answer gives three advantages. Specific examples are given, which is a good way to show that you understand the topic. The use of 'however' is a good way of moving to the disadvantages.

## Now try this

An aluminium alloy commonly used to make aircraft contains 4.4% copper, with smaller amounts of other elements. Use the information in the table, and what you know about alloys, to explain why this aluminium alloy is used for aircraft rather than pure aluminium or steel. *(6 marks)*

| Metal | Density in g/cm$^3$ | Relative strength |
|---|---|---|
| aluminium | 2.7 | 1.0 |
| aluminium alloy | 2.8 | 4.7 |
| steel | 7.8 | 11.8 |

> Think about the properties an aircraft material should have. What properties, in addition to those given, would an aluminium alloy need and why?

# Atomic structure and isotopes

## Representing atoms

Atoms can be represented like this:

mass number —— $^{23}_{11}$Na —— chemical symbol
atomic number ——

This is the full symbol for sodium, Na.

## Particles in atoms

The table shows the relative masses of the particles in an atom.

| Name of particle | Relative mass |
|---|---|
| proton | 1 |
| neutron | 1 |
| electron | very small |

## Numbers

The MASS NUMBER of an atom is the total number of protons and neutrons in an atom. The ATOMIC NUMBER of an atom is the number of protons in an atom.

These two numbers can be used to work out the number of protons, neutrons and electrons in an atom.

- Number of protons = atomic number
- Number of neutrons = mass number − atomic number
- Number of electrons = atomic number

For $^{23}_{11}$Na:
- Number of protons = 11
- Number of neutrons = 23 − 11 = 12
- Number of electrons = 11

## Worked example

Two isotopes of chlorine are shown below:
$^{35}_{17}$Cl and $^{37}_{17}$Cl

Explain what isotopes are. *(4 marks)*

Isotopes are atoms of the same element with the same number of protons and electrons, but different numbers of neutrons.

You can recognise **isotopes** of an element because they will have the same atomic number but different mass numbers.

These atoms both have 17 protons and electrons, but:
$^{35}_{17}$Cl has 35 − 17 = 18 neutrons
$^{37}_{17}$Cl has 37 − 17 = 20 neutrons
The answer could have included this information.

## Now try this

**1** Tick (✓) **two** correct statements about particles in atoms. *(2 marks)*

| Statement | Tick (✓) |
|---|---|
| electrons are much heavier than protons | |
| protons and neutrons have the same mass | |
| electrons have a very small mass compared with neutrons | |
| protons are heavier than neutrons | |

**2** Three atoms are represented here: $^{1}_{1}$H   $^{2}_{1}$H   $^{3}_{1}$H

Explain why they are isotopes of the same element. *(4 marks)*

Had a look ☐   Nearly there ☐   Nailed it! ☐   **CHEMISTRY 2.3.1**

# Relative formula mass

## Relative formula mass
The RELATIVE FORMULA MASS of a substance is all the relative atomic masses of all the atoms shown in its formula added together.

Relative formula mass has the symbol $M_r$ and it has no units – it is just a number.

## Moles
The relative formula mass of a substance, in grams, is known as one MOLE of that substance. For example, the formula of oxygen gas is $O_2$. Each molecule contains two oxygen atoms.
($A_r$ of O = 16)
$M_r$ of $O_2$ = 16 + 16 = 32
32 g of oxygen gas, $O_2$, is one mole of oxygen.

**Relative atomic masses** ($A_r$ values) will normally be given to you in an exam question. If you need to look them up, they are on the Periodic Table given in the exam. Use the greater number in each box.

(16) O oxygen 8

### Worked example (target G-E)

(a) Calculate the relative formula mass, $M_r$, of water, $H_2O$. *(1 mark)*
   ($A_r$ of H = 1, $A_r$ of O = 16)
   $M_r$ of $H_2O$ = 1 + 1 + 16 = 18

(b) What is the mass of one mole of water? *(1 mark)*
   18 g

The 3 next to the O means that there are 3 oxygen atoms. So in the formula $CaCO_3$, there are:
- 1 × Ca
- 1 × C
- 3 × O

### Worked example (target D-C)

(a) Calculate the relative formula mass, $M_r$, of calcium carbonate, $CaCO_3$. *(1 mark)*
   ($A_r$ of Ca = 40, $A_r$ of C = 12, $A_r$ of O = 16)
   $M_r$ of $CaCO_3$ = 40 + 12 + 16 + 16 + 16
                    = 100

(b) What is the mass of one mole of $CaCO_3$? *(1 mark)*
   100 g

You can also use multiplication to get the same answer:
$M_r$ of $CaCO_3$ = 40 + 12 + (3 × 16)
                 = 52 + 48 = 100

### EXAM ALERT!
Don't confuse relative formula mass and moles. Moles have units (usually grams). For example, the formula mass of water is 18, but the mass of one mole is 18 grams.

Students have struggled with exam questions similar to this – **be prepared!**

## Now try this

Use these relative atomic masses to answer the questions:
H = 1, C = 12, N = 14, O = 16, Na = 23, Mg = 24, S = 32

**1** (target G-E) Calculate the relative formula masses in the following substances.
(a) oxygen, $O_2$ *(1 mark)*
(b) carbon dioxide, $CO_2$ *(1 mark)*
(c) sodium hydroxide, NaOH *(1 mark)*

**2** (target D-C) Calculate the relative formula masses in the following compounds.
(a) sodium carbonate, $Na_2CO_3$ *(1 mark)*
(b) magnesium sulfate, $MgSO_4$ *(1 mark)*
(c) ethane, $C_2H_6$ *(1 mark)*

# Paper chromatography

## Paper chromatography
Artificial colourings may be added to food to improve its appearance. PAPER CHROMATOGRAPHY can be used to detect and identify artificial colours.

## Carrying out paper chromatography
To set up paper chromatography:
- draw a pencil line near the bottom of the paper
- add spots of colourings to the line
- put the paper into a chromatography tank with a solvent at the bottom and below the line.

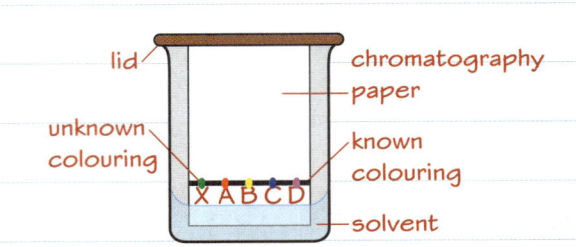

To analyse paper chromatography:
- take the paper out before the solvent reaches the top
- examine the spots on the chromatogram.

Two coloured spots on a **chromatogram** are likely to be the same substance if they:
- are the same colour
- travel the same distance up the paper.

## Worked example (G-E)

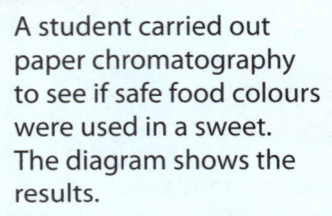

A student carried out paper chromatography to see if safe food colours were used in a sweet. The diagram shows the results.

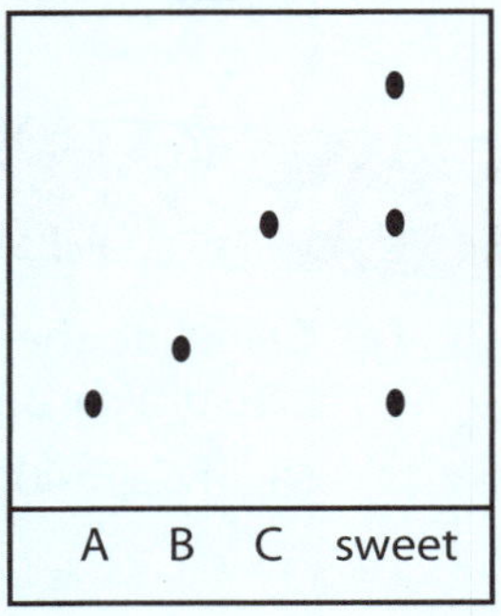

(a) How many different colours were present in the sweet? *(1 mark)*

Three

There are three spots above where the sweet's colouring was added. Remember that they will not be coloured on the exam paper.

(b) Colours A, B and C are safe. Explain whether the sweet is safe to eat. *(2 marks)*

You cannot be sure because not all the spots match, and one could be unsafe.

The sweet contains the safe colours A and C, but not the safe colour B. However, it contains a colour that travelled higher than A, B or C. You cannot tell from a chromatogram whether this colour is safe.

## Now try this

**1** (G-E) The diagram shows the results of a paper chromatography experiment.

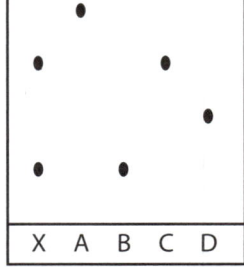

(a) How many colours were present in substance X? *(1 mark)*

(b) Which colours (A, B, C or D) were present in substance X? *(1 mark)*

**2** (D-C) (a) Suggest why pencil, rather than pen, is used to draw the line on chromatography paper. *(1 mark)*

(b) Suggest why a lid is needed for the tank during paper chromatography. *(1 mark)*

Had a look ☐   Nearly there ☐   Nailed it! ☐   **CHEMISTRY 2.3.2**

# Gas chromatography

GAS CHROMATOGRAPHY linked to MASS SPECTROSCOPY (GC-MS) is an example of an instrumental method used to analyse substances.

## Gas chromatography

Gas chromatography (GC) allows a mixture of compounds to be separated. In GC, a circular column that contains solid material is used instead of paper. The column is fitted into a temperature-controlled oven.

- cylinder of carrier gas
- detector
- column in oven
- gas chromatogram

A gas carries the different substances through the column.

The different substances travel at different speeds through the column, so they become separated.

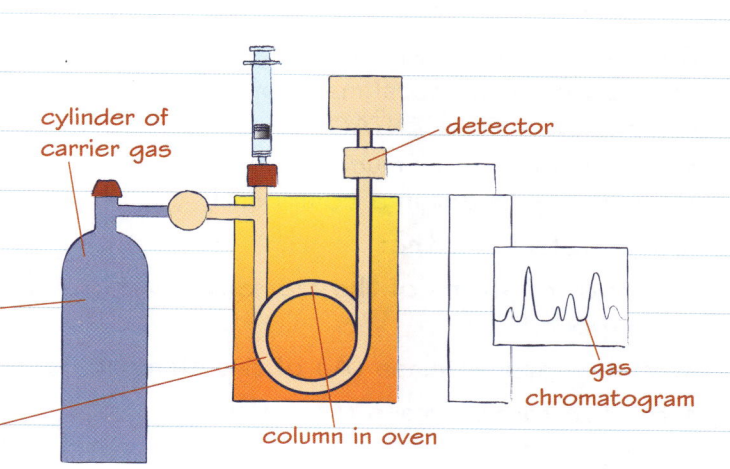

## The gas chromatograph

The output from gas chromatography is a GAS CHROMATOGRAM. The RETENTION TIME is the time taken for a substance to pass through the column to the detector.

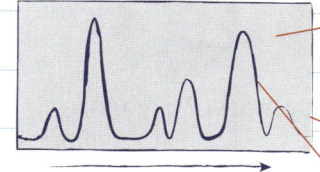

increasing retention time →

The number of peaks shows the number of compounds present in the sample.

The position of a peak shows its retention time.

There are six different substances in this example. The peak on the right shows the substance that travels slowest through the column.

## Worked example

**target D-C**

Gas chromatography is an instrumental method of analysis. Give **two** advantages of using gas chromatography instead of paper chromatography to analyse substances.   *(2 marks)*

Gas chromatography is quick and accurate, whereas paper chromatography is slow and it can be difficult to measure the distance travelled by the spots.

There are other instrumental methods of analysis. They are used to detect and identify elements and compounds in substances. The output from the gas chromatography column can be linked to a **mass spectrometer**. This machine can identify the different substances.

Instrumental methods are also sensitive, so they can detect tiny amounts. This is useful when the sample amount is very small.

## Now try this

**target G-E**

1. (a) What does gas chromatography do to the substances in a sample?   *(1 mark)*
   (b) What information does the number of peaks on a gas chromatograph provide?   *(1 mark)*
   (c) What is the 'retention time' for a substance in gas chromatography?   *(1 mark)*
   (d) What does a mass spectrometer do?   *(1 mark)*
   (e) What is GC-MS?   *(1 mark)*

# Percentage composition

## Percentage composition by mass

The atoms of each element in a compound contribute to the total mass of the compound. A PERCENTAGE COMPOSITION is a measure of how much of a particular element is present in a compound.

You need to know the:
- number of atoms of the element in the compound ← The chemical formula shows this.
- relative atomic mass ($A_r$) of the element ← Given in the question.
- relative formula mass ($M_r$) of the compound. ← Calculated from the formula and $A_r$ values.

Different atoms have different masses, so they do not contribute equally to the total mass. Hydrogen atoms only contribute 11% of the mass of a water molecule, $H_2O$.

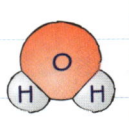

### Worked example (D-C)

Calculate the percentage by mass of oxygen in sodium hydroxide, NaOH. *(3 marks)*
(Relative atomic masses: Na = 23, O = 16, H = 1)

$M_r$ of NaOH = 23 + 16 + 1 = 40

% by mass of O = $\dfrac{\text{mass of oxygen} \times 100}{M_r}$

= (1 × 16)/40 × 100%
= 40%

*Calculate the $M_r$ first.*

*There is only one oxygen atom in the formula, which is why (1 × 16) is shown.*

### Worked example (D-C)

Calculate the percentage by mass of oxygen in sulfur dioxide, $SO_2$. *(3 marks)*
(Relative atomic masses: S = 32, O = 16)

$M_r$ of $SO_2$ = 32 + 16 + 16 = 64
% by mass of O = (2 × 16)/64 × 100%
= 32/64 × 100%
= 50%

*Calculate the $M_r$ first. This could have been done using multiplication: 32 + (2 × 16) = 64*

*There are two oxygen atoms in the formula, which is why (2 × 16) is shown here.*

### Now try this (D-C)

Use these relative atomic masses to answer the questions: H = 1, C = 12, N = 14, O = 16

1. Calculate the percentage by mass of carbon in methane, $CH_4$. *(3 marks)*
2. Calculate the percentage by mass of nitrogen in ammonia, $NH_3$. *(3 marks)*
3. Calculate the percentage by mass of oxygen in carbon dioxide. *(3 marks)*
4. Calculate the percentage by mass of nitrogen in ammonium nitrate, $NH_4NO_3$. *(3 marks)*

Had a look ☐   Nearly there ☐   Nailed it! ☐   **CHEMISTRY 2.3.3**

# Reaction yields

The amount of a product obtained in a chemical process is called its YIELD.

## Maximum theoretical yield

In a chemical reaction:
- no atoms are gained
- no atoms are lost.

For a given mass of reactants, it is only possible to make a certain maximum mass of products. This is the THEORETICAL YIELD.

> The theoretical yield can be calculated using the balanced symbol equation for the reaction, and the relative masses of the substances involved. You will not be asked to do this at Foundation level.

## Actual yield

The ACTUAL YIELD is usually less than the theoretical yield.

**REASONS FOR NOT GETTING THE THEORETICAL YIELD:**
- The reaction may be reversible, so it may not go to completion.
- Some of the product may be lost while separating it from the reaction mixer.
- There may be other reactions going on, so the reactants may produce other products (by-products) as well.

## Worked example (target D-C)

When copper(II) carbonate is heated, it decomposes to form copper(II) oxide and carbon dioxide. The table shows the results from four experiments.

| Experiment | Theoretical yield in g | Actual yield in g |
|---|---|---|
| 1 | 0.5 | 0.4 |
| 2 | 1.0 | 0.8 |
| 3 | 1.5 | 1.2 |
| 4 | 2.0 | 1.2 |

**(a)** Suggest **one** reason for the difference between the theoretical yield and actual yield. *(1 mark)*

Some of the copper(II) carbonate may not have decomposed to form copper(II) oxide.

**(b)** Explain which experiment gave an anomalous result. *(2 marks)*

Experiment 4 was anomalous because the actual yield did not follow the trend. For 2.0 g of copper(II) carbonate you would expect 1.6 g, but it was much less than this.

> The **percentage yield** for experiments 1, 2 and 3 is 80%. The percentage yield is the actual yield compared to the theoretical yield, given as a percentage:
> - 0% means that no expected product was obtained.
> - 100% means that all of the expected product was obtained.

## Now try this

**1** (target G-E) What is the yield of a product? *(1 mark)*

**2** (target D-C) **(a)** How is the actual yield usually different from the theoretical yield? *(1 mark)*
**(b)** Give **two** reasons for this difference. *(2 marks)*

# CHEMISTRY 2.3.3

Had a look ☐   Nearly there ☐   Nailed it! ☐

# Reversible reactions

Some reactions are REVERSIBLE. This means that the products can react to make the original reactants.

## Equations

Many reactions are not reversible. They go to completion and the products cannot react with each other.

$$A + B \rightarrow C + D$$

the reactants — the products

Reversible reactions are shown with a split arrow pointing in both directions:

$$A + B \rightleftharpoons C + D$$

shows that the reaction is reversible

## A reversible reaction

Ammonium chloride is a white solid. It breaks down when heated, forming ammonia and hydrogen chloride gases:

ammonium chloride → ammonia + hydrogen chloride

When the products cool down, they react together to form ammonium chloride:

ammonia + hydrogen chloride → ammonium chloride

Overall, the reaction is shown like this:

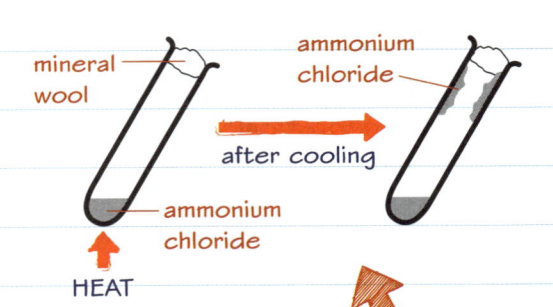

ammonium chloride ⇌ ammonia + hydrogen chloride

> The mineral wool stops ammonia and hydrogen chloride escaping. Ammonium chloride forms where the test tube is cool.

## Worked example (target G-E)

Hydrated copper sulfate crystals change when heated:

hydrated copper sulfate (blue) ⇌ anhydrous copper sulfate (white) + water

Describe what you would see when hydrated copper sulfate is heated. *(2 marks)*

The crystals will turn from blue to white, and steam will be given off.

> Remember that the symbol ⇌ means that the reaction is reversible.
> The chemical formula for hydrated copper sulfate includes water. For example: $CuSO_4.5H_2O$

> The answer includes both colours (before and after).

## Now try this

**1** State what this symbol means: ⇌   *(1 mark)*   (target G-E)

**2** Hydrated copper sulfate crystals change from blue to white when heated:

hydrated copper sulfate (blue) ⇌ anhydrous copper sulfate (white) + water

Describe how anhydrous copper sulfate crystals could be used as a test for water.   *(2 marks)*   (target D-C)

Had a look ☐  Nearly there ☐  Nailed it! ☐   **CHEMISTRY 2.4.1**

# Rates of reaction

Reactions happen at different rates.

*Explosions are very fast reactions.*

*Rusting is a very slow reaction.*

## Measuring rates

The RATE of a reaction can be found by measuring:
- the amount of reactant used over time, or
- the amount of product made over time.

$$\text{rate} = \frac{\text{amount of reactant used}}{\text{time}}$$

$$\text{rate} = \frac{\text{amount of product formed}}{\text{time}}$$

## Graphs

The amount of product formed increases as time goes by. The reaction is finished when the line becomes horizontal.

The amount of reactant left decreases as time goes by. The reaction is finished when the line becomes horizontal.

### Worked example  target D-C

*AQA SKILL Interpret Page 101*

A student carried out an experiment to investigate the rate of reaction between magnesium and hydrochloric acid.

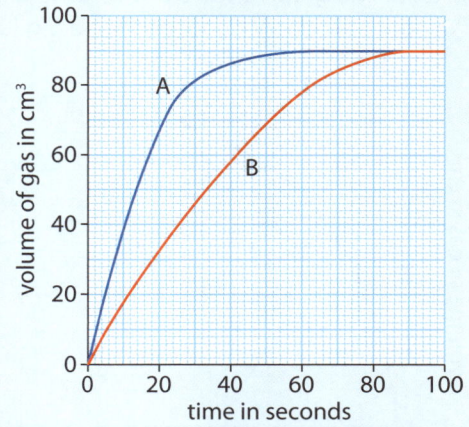

Use the graph to describe **one** way in which reactions A and B are different, and **two** ways in which they are similar. *(3 marks)*

The rate of reaction A is greater than the rate of reaction B. The same volume of gas is produced in both reactions, and the rates of both reactions decrease as time goes by.

The line for reaction A is steeper than the line for reaction B. The steeper the line, the greater the rate of reaction. Reactions usually start off quickly and gradually slow down until they stop.

### Now try this

**target G-E**
1. In general, how can the rate of a reaction be measured? *(2 marks)*

Look at the graph in the Worked Example to help you answer these questions.

**target D-C**
2. Describe, as fully as you can, how the rate of reaction A changes over time. *(2 marks)*

**target D-C**
3. (a) How long does it take for reaction B to stop? *(1 mark)*
   (b) How much gas is formed in reaction B? *(1 mark)*
   (c) Use your answers to parts (a) and (b) to calculate the average rate of reaction for reaction B. *(2 marks)*

51

# Changing rates 1

## Colliding particles

For a reaction to happen:
- reactant particles must collide with each other, and
- the collision must have enough energy.

A SUCCESSFUL COLLISION has enough energy for a reaction to happen.

> The minimum amount of energy particles need to react is called the **activation energy**.

> The greater the rate of successful collisions, the greater the rate of reaction.

## Increasing the temperature

Increasing the temperature increases the rate of reaction. This is because:
- the reacting particles move more quickly
- they collide more frequently
- more of the particles have the activation energy (or more).

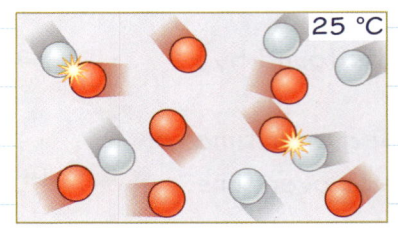

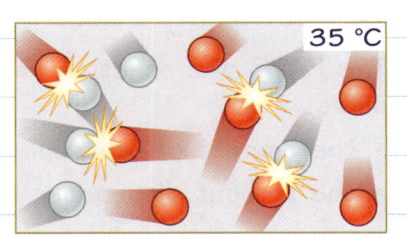

### Worked example

Carbon dioxide gas is produced when calcium carbonate reacts with hydrochloric acid. The graph shows the volume of gas produced every minute when a 5 g lump of calcium carbonate is used.

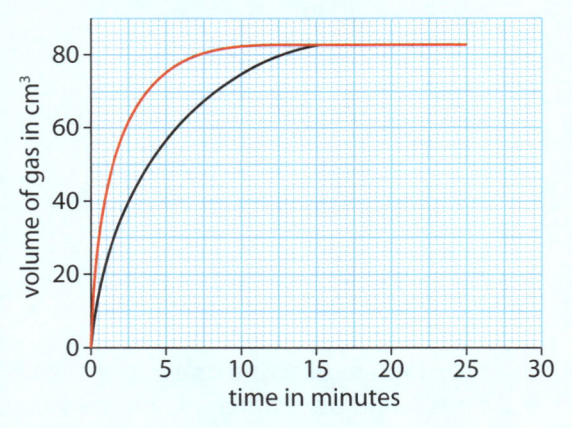

(a) Draw a line on the graph to show the line you would expect if the reaction were carried out under the same conditions, but with 5 g of powdered calcium carbonate. *(2 marks)*

(b) Explain any differences you may have drawn. *(2 marks)*

The powder has a bigger surface area, so the frequency of collisions is greater. This increases the rate of reaction.

> The conditions were the same, with the same mass of calcium carbonate, so the graph lines finish at the same volume. The line for the powder starts at the origin, but is steeper and to the left of the other line.

### Now try this

1. Calcium reacts with dilute acid. Tick (✓) **two** correct methods to increase the rate of reaction. *(2 marks)*

| Method | Tick (✓) |
| --- | --- |
| increase the temperature of the acid | |
| use a less concentrated acid | |
| use smaller pieces of calcium | |
| use a smaller volume of acid | |

2. Explain as fully as you can why increasing the temperature changes the rate of reaction. *(4 marks)*

Had a look ☐   Nearly there ☐   Nailed it! ☐   **CHEMISTRY 2.4.1**

# Changing rates 2

## Increasing collisions

The rate of reaction can be increased by increasing the frequency of collisions. In addition to increasing the temperature, this can be done by:
- increasing the concentration of reactants in solution
- increasing the pressure of reacting gases.

low concentration — high concentration (more particles in the same volume)
acid particles
marble chip meet and react — marble chip

### EXAM ALERT!

Increasing the concentration or pressure only increases the frequency of collisions. Unlike increasing the temperature, it does not increase the energy of the collisions.

> Students have struggled with this topic in recent exams – **be prepared!**

## Using catalysts

A CATALYST is a substance that changes the rate of a chemical reaction without being used up during the reaction. Different reactions need different catalysts.

> Catalysts are important in the chemical industry. When they increase the rate of the chemical reaction used in a process, this reduces the cost of the process.

### Worked example (D-C)

Methanal is used in the chemical industry. It is made from methanol, using silver as a catalyst. Silver is an expensive metal. Evaluate the use of silver as a catalyst in the manufacture of methanal. *(3 marks)*

> Different reactions need different catalysts, and sometimes only one will work well.

Catalysts speed up reactions and lower the temperature needed, reducing costs. Silver is expensive, but it is a catalyst, so it will be needed in small amounts and will never be used up. It is worth using silver as a catalyst.

> The answer explains why the use of catalysts reduces costs.

> Other expensive metals may be used as catalysts for chemical reactions, such as gold or platinum.

## Now try this

1. **(G-E)** Nitrogen gas and hydrogen gas react together to make ammonia. Give **three** ways in which the rate of reaction could be increased. *(3 marks)*

2. **(D-C)** Vegetable oils are processed for use in margarine by reacting them with hydrogen gas. Nickel is added to the reaction mixture but all of it can be removed afterwards.
   (a) Explain why nickel is added to the reaction mixture. *(3 marks)*
   (b) The reaction is normally carried out at 60 °C. Suggest **one** reason why a higher temperature should be used and **one** reason why a higher temperature should not be used. *(2 marks)*

3. **(D-C)** Explain, in terms of particles, why concentrated hydrochloric acid reacts more quickly with magnesium than dilute acid does. *(2 marks)*

# Chemistry six mark question 2

There will be one 6 mark question on your exam paper, which will be marked for quality of *written communication* as well as scientific knowledge. This means that you need to apply your scientific knowledge, present your answer in a logical and organised way, and make sure that your spelling, grammar and punctuation are as good as you can make them.

## Worked example

Hydrogen fuel can be made from fossil fuels using two processes.

Process 1 uses natural gas and steam at 850 °C:

methane + steam → carbon dioxide + hydrogen

One methane molecule is needed to produce four hydrogen molecules in the reaction.

Process 2 uses coal and steam at 400 °C:

carbon + steam → carbon monoxide + hydrogen

One carbon atom is needed to produce one hydrogen molecule in the reaction.

Evaluate the two methods of making hydrogen.

(6 marks)

Process 1 needs a higher temperature than Process 2. This will mean that it will need more fuel to produce the heat needed. This may make the process more expensive and produce more waste. On the other hand, Process 1 makes more hydrogen from natural gas than Process 2 does from coal.

Process 2 produces carbon monoxide, which is a toxic substance. However, Process 1 produces carbon dioxide, which is a greenhouse gas. Overall, I think Process 1 is better because it makes more hydrogen.

### Evaluate

If you are asked to evaluate two processes, discuss the advantages and disadvantages of each process, and then come to a conclusion about which one is better.

The answer discusses a disadvantage of Process 1 and how that might matter. This is then balanced by an advantage of Process 1.

It would be fine to say that Process 2 was better as long as you could justify your conclusion.

If fossil fuels are used to provide the heat needed, both processes will produce carbon dioxide. Additional greenhouse gases in the atmosphere lead to global warming.

## Now try this

A manufacturer is developing self-heating food cans. These rely on exothermic reactions to heat up the food. In Process 1, magnesium powder reacts with water to produce magnesium hydroxide and hydrogen, releasing 1.3 kJ per gram of magnesium. In Process 2, calcium chloride dissolves in water to produce calcium chloride solution, releasing 1.1 kJ per gram of calcium chloride. Evaluate the two ways to release heat for a self-heating can.

(6 marks)

Had a look ☐   Nearly there ☐   Nailed it! ☐   **CHEMISTRY 2.5.1**

# Energy changes

When chemical reactions happen, energy is transferred to the surroundings or from the surroundings.

## Exothermic and endothermic reactions

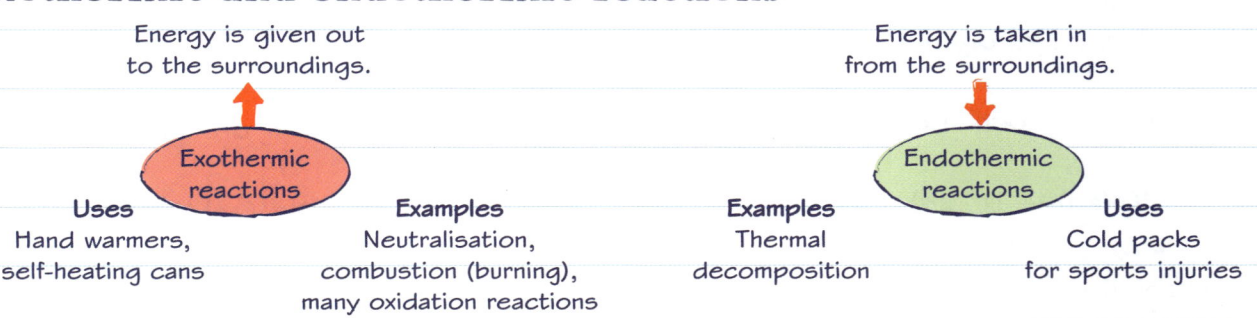

Energy is given out to the surroundings. → **Exothermic reactions**

**Uses**: Hand warmers, self-heating cans
**Examples**: Neutralisation, combustion (burning), many oxidation reactions

Energy is taken in from the surroundings. → **Endothermic reactions**

**Examples**: Thermal decomposition
**Uses**: Cold packs for sports injuries

## Reversible reactions

In reversible reactions:
- one direction is exothermic and the other one is endothermic
- the same amount of energy is transferred (either to the surroundings or from them).

For example:

hydrated copper sulfate $\underset{\text{exothermic}}{\overset{\text{endothermic}}{\rightleftharpoons}}$ anhydrous copper sulfate + water

> A thermometer could be used to measure the temperature change. The reaction mixture gets hotter in exothermic reactions and colder in endothermic reactions.

### Worked example (D-C)

A sport injury pack consists of a bag of ammonium nitrate, with a smaller bag of water inside. The outer bag is squeezed to burst the inner bag. The pack is shaken so that the ammonium nitrate dissolves in water and gets cold.

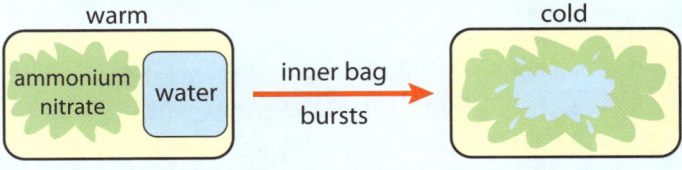

[warm: ammonium nitrate + water] — inner bag bursts → [cold]

Explain why the pack gets cold. *(2 marks)*

*An endothermic change happens when ammonium nitrate dissolves in water. Heat energy is taken in from the surroundings, making the pack cold.*

> The bag is shaken so that the contents mix quickly.

### Now try this

**G-E**
1. The reaction between aluminium and iron oxide is highly exothermic. What does **exothermic** mean? *(2 marks)*
2. When electricity is passed through water, the water decomposes to form hydrogen and oxygen. Explain whether this reaction is exothermic or endothermic. *(2 marks)*

**D-C**
3. Hydrated copper sulfate gives off water and becomes anhydrous copper sulfate when it is heated continuously. The reaction is reversible. Explain why anhydrous copper sulfate becomes hot when water is added to it. *(3 marks)*

# Acids and alkalis

## Acids

ACIDS have these properties:
- a pH below 7
- they release hydrogen ions, $H^+(aq)$, into solution.

For example, hydrochloric acid releases $H^+$ ions:

$$HCl(aq) \rightarrow H^+(aq) + Cl^-(aq)$$

(aq) in the symbol equation is a **state symbol**: (aq) means aqueous (dissolved in water), (s) means solid, (l) means liquid and (g) means gas.

## Alkalis

ALKALIS have these properties:
- a pH above 7
- they release hydroxide ions, $OH^-(aq)$, into solution.

For example, sodium hydroxide releases $OH^-$ ions:

$$NaOH(aq) \rightarrow Na^+(aq) + OH^-(aq)$$

A **base** is a substance, usually a metal oxide or a metal hydroxide, that can neutralise acids. Soluble hydroxides are called alkalis.

## The pH scale

The pH SCALE is a measure of the ACIDITY or ALKALINITY of a solution (how acidic or alkaline it is). It goes from 0 to 14. NEUTRAL solutions are pH 7.

INDICATORS are substances that have different colours, depending on their pH. Universal indicator solution or paper is often used to estimate the pH of a solution.

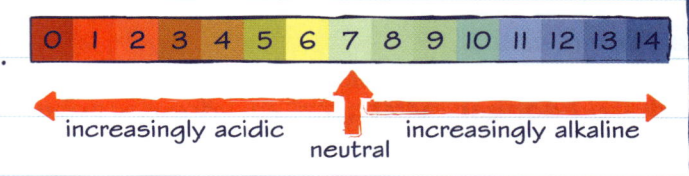

The colour produced by the indicator is matched to a colour chart, which shows the pH for each colour.

### Worked example (D-C)

In neutralisation reactions, hydrogen ions $H^+(aq)$ react with hydroxide ions $OH^-(aq)$ to produce water. Complete this equation, including the correct state symbols. *(2 marks)*

$$H^+(aq) + OH^-(aq) \rightarrow H_2O(l)$$

Hydrogen ions come from the acid and hydroxide ions from the alkali.

Water is produced in neutralisation reactions. The state symbol (l) shows that it is a liquid.

### Now try this

1. **(G-E)**
   (a) What is a **base**? *(1 mark)*
   (b) What is an **alkali**? *(1 mark)*

2. Acids and alkalis release ions in solution. Give the names and symbols of the ion that makes a solution (a) acidic and (b) alkaline. *(2 marks)*

3. **(D-C)** Phenolphthalein is an indicator. It is colourless but becomes pink above pH 8.
   (a) What is an **indicator**? *(1 mark)*
   (b) Describe the colour of phenolphthalein in hydrochloric acid. *(2 marks)*

4. Explain what happens during a neutralisation reaction. Use a balanced symbol equation, including state symbols, to help you. *(4 marks)*

Had a look ☐    Nearly there ☐    Nailed it! ☐    **CHEMISTRY 2.6.1**

# Making salts

Soluble salts can be made by reacting acids with alkalis, then crystallising the salt solution to produce solid salts.

## Naming salts

In general: acid + alkali → salt + water

The actual salt made depends on:
- the metal in the alkali
- the acid used.

For example:
hydrochloric acid + sodium hydroxide → sodium chloride + water

| Acid used | Type of salt |
|---|---|
| hydrochloric acid | chloride |
| nitric acid | nitrate |
| sulfuric acid | sulfate |

## Steps for making salts

The flow chart shows the main steps needed to make a soluble salt from an acid and an alkali.

| Put some alkali into a flask and add a few drops of indicator. | → | Add acid drop by drop until the indicator changes colour. | → | Add carbon powder to remove the indicator, and then filter. | → | Evaporate the filtrate to leave solid salt behind. |

The volumes of acid and alkali needed to produce a neutral solution can be recorded. These volumes can then be mixed without an indicator, cutting out the need for the third step.

## Worked example (target D-C)

Ammonium nitrate is a soluble salt used in fertilisers.

(a) Name **two** substances that will react together to make ammonium nitrate. *(2 marks)*

Ammonia solution and nitric acid.

(b) State how you could show that the substances have neutralised each other. *(1 mark)*

Use an indicator.

*Ammonia dissolves in water to make an alkaline solution. This produces **ammonium salts** when it reacts with acids. These are important as **fertilisers**, which provide minerals needed for plants to grow well.*

*The name of a suitable indicator could be given instead.*

## Now try this

**target G-E**

1. Name the salts produced by the following mixtures of acid and alkali:
   (a) potassium hydroxide and hydrochloric acid *(1 mark)*
   (b) sodium hydroxide and nitric acid *(1 mark)*
   (c) ammonia solution and sulfuric acid. *(1 mark)*

**target D-C**

2. Describe how to make a dry sample of sodium chloride, a soluble salt, from a suitable acid and alkali. *(4 marks)*

### EXAM ALERT!

You should know how to name different salts.

Students have struggled with exam questions similar to this – **be prepared!**

*In your answer, mention the names of the acid and alkali needed, how you will make a neutral sodium chloride solution and then produce the dry sample from it.*

# Making soluble salts

Soluble salts can be made by reacting acids with metals, or with insoluble bases, and then crystallising the salt solution.

## Reactions with metals

In general:

acid + metal → salt + hydrogen

You cannot use this method with all metals.

✗ Copper and other metals that are less reactive than hydrogen are not reactive enough.

✗ Sodium and other very reactive metals are too reactive for it to be safe to do.

## Reactions with insoluble bases

In general, for metal oxides and metal hydroxides:

acid + base → salt + water

When making a soluble salt, an **excess** of metal or base is used. This is enough to neutralise the acid and have some metal or base left over. This can be filtered off.

## Steps for making salts

The flow chart shows the main steps needed to make solid copper sulfate from copper oxide (an insoluble base) and sulfuric acid.

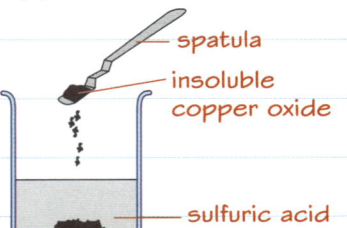

**1** Add excess base to the acid.

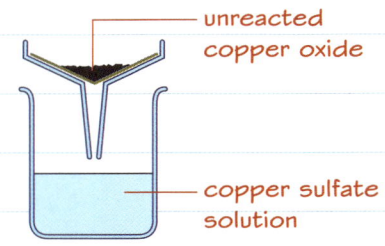

**2** Filter to remove unreacted copper oxide.

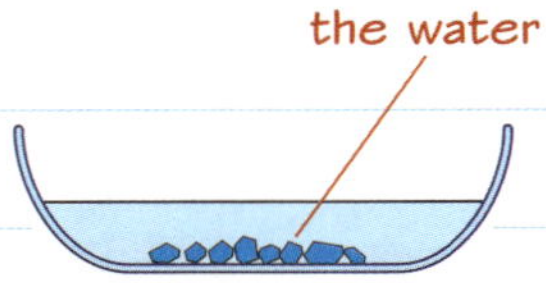

**3** Crystallise the copper sulfate solution by heating it or leaving it to stand in a warm place.

The same method works for reacting a metal with an acid.

## Worked example

Describe how a sample of dry copper chloride could be produced from a suitable acid and insoluble base. Include the names of the substances needed in your answer. (3 marks)

Add copper oxide powder to hydrochloric acid until an excess of powder remains, then filter. Evaporate the water from the copper chloride solution to leave dry crystals behind.

## Now try this

1. Explain why potassium sulfate is made by reacting sulfuric acid with potassium hydroxide, rather than with potassium metal. (1 mark)

2. Zinc chloride can be made from hydrochloric acid and an insoluble solid.
   (a) Name a suitable insoluble solid. (1 mark)
   (b) Briefly describe a method that could be used to make zinc chloride. (3 marks)

3. (a) State the reactants needed to make magnesium nitrate from an insoluble base. (2 marks)
   (b) Write a word equation for the reaction. (1 mark)

Had a look ☐    Nearly there ☐    Nailed it! ☐    **CHEMISTRY 2.6.1**

# Making insoluble salts

## Precipitation reactions

SOLUBLE substances dissolve in water, while INSOLUBLE substances do not. Insoluble salts can be made by mixing two suitable solutions together. The ions in these solutions combine to form an insoluble salt. This appears as a PRECIPITATE, which makes the mixture look cloudy rather than clear. For example:

$$\text{silver nitrate} + \text{sodium iodide} \rightarrow \text{sodium nitrate} + \text{silver iodide}$$
$$AgNO_3(aq) + NaI(aq) \rightarrow NaNO_3(aq) + AgI(s)$$

## Using precipitates

Precipitation reactions can be used to:
- remove unwanted ions from solutions (for example, to treat drinking water or waste water)
- make insoluble salts (as shown in the diagrams).

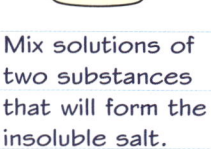

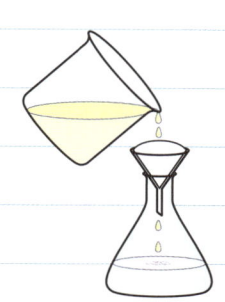

**1** Mix solutions of two substances that will form the insoluble salt.

**2** Filter the mixture. The insoluble salt will be trapped in the filter paper.

**3** Wash the salt with pure water.

**4** Leave the salt to dry on the filter paper. It could be dried in an oven.

## Worked example (D-C)

Barium sulfate is an insoluble salt. Name **two** substances that could be used to make it. *(2 marks)*

Barium nitrate and sodium sulfate.

> All nitrates, and all sodium salts, are soluble. So to make an insoluble salt 'XY', choose 'X nitrate' and 'sodium Y' as your suitable substances.

## Now try this

**(G-E)** 1 Some industrial processes form waste water that contains harmful cadmium ions. Precipitation is one way to remove these ions before the waste water is released into rivers:

$$CdCl_2(aq) + Na_2CO_3(aq) \rightarrow 2NaCl(aq) + CdCO_3(s)$$

(a) State what happens in a precipitation reaction. *(1 mark)*
(b) Identify the precipitate and explain your answer. *(2 marks)*

**(D-C)** 2 Name **two** solutions you can mix to make calcium carbonate, an insoluble salt. *(2 marks)*

**CHEMISTRY 2.7.1**   Had a look ☐   Nearly there ☐   Nailed it! ☐

# Using electricity

ELECTROLYSIS is a process that uses electricity to break down ionic compounds, forming other useful substances. It can also be used to coat objects with metals.

## Electrodes and moving ions

During electrolysis positively charged ions are attracted to the negative electrode and move to it.

Negatively charged ions are attracted to the positive electrode and move to it during electrolysis.

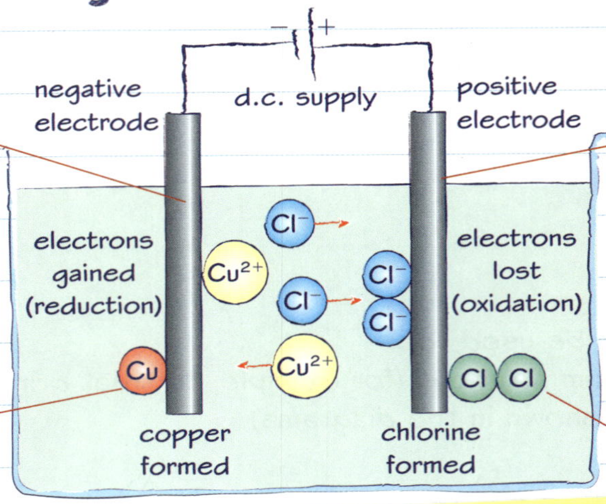

Positively charged ions gain electrons and are REDUCED.

Remember 'oil rig': **o**xidation **i**s **l**oss of electrons. **r**eduction **i**s **g**ain of electrons.

Negatively charged ions lose electrons and are OXIDISED.

*Electrolysis of copper chloride solution*

### Worked example (target D–C)

The **electrolyte** is the substance that conducts electricity during electrolysis.

Electrolysis may be used to electroplate steel cutlery with a thin coating of silver.

**(a)** Name a suitable electrolyte for this process. *(1 mark)*

Silver nitrate solution.

**(b)** Explain whether the steel cutlery should be the positive electrode, or the negative electrode. *(2 marks)*

It should be the negative electrode. This is because metal ions are positively charged, so they will be attracted to it.

**(c)** Name a suitable substance for the other electrode. *(1 mark)*

Silver.

The positive electrode should be made from the electroplating metal.

## Moving charge

The ions in an electrolyte are charged particles. An electric current will only pass through the electrolyte if they are free to move from place to place.

✓ Ions can move about in liquids.
✓ Ions can move about in solutions.
✗ Ions cannot move about in solids.

### Now try this

**(target G–E)**

1. To which electrode do copper ions, $Cu^{2+}$, move during electrolysis? Explain your answer. *(2 marks)*
2. Explain why molten lead bromide is an electrolyte but solid lead bromide is not. *(2 marks)*

**(target D–C)**

3. Electroplating can be used to plate copper onto machine parts. Describe how this process can be carried out. *(4 marks)*

In your answer, state what the two electrodes should be and include a suitable electrolyte.

Had a look ☐  Nearly there ☐  Nailed it! ☐   **CHEMISTRY 2.7.1**

# Useful substances from electrolysis

## Manufacture of aluminium

Aluminium is manufactured by the electrolysis of aluminium oxide.

Aluminium oxide is insoluble so it must be molten for its ions to move about. However, it has a high melting point, which makes the process very expensive.

## Cryolite

CRYOLITE is used to reduce the temperature (and energy cost) for the process. This substance has a lower melting point and aluminium oxide dissolves in it. The electrolyte is a molten mixture of cryolite and aluminium oxide.

Diagram labels:
- carbon blocks (positive electrodes)
- molten mixture of aluminium oxide and cryolite
- oxygen forms
- steel casing
- carbon lining (the negative electrode)
- molten aluminium forms
- aluminium poured off
- oxide ions move to positive electrode, lose electrons and form oxygen
- aluminium ions move to negative electrode, gain electrons and form aluminium

The oxygen produced reacts with the carbon of the positive electrodes, producing carbon dioxide. The positive electrodes gradually burn away and must be replaced every two weeks.

### Worked example (target D-C)

The electrolysis of sodium chloride solution is an important industrial process.

**(a)** Name the solution formed during electrolysis, and give **one** use for it. *(2 marks)*

Sodium hydroxide solution is produced. It is used in the manufacture of soap.

**(b)** Name the **two** gases produced from the electrolysis of sodium chloride solution, and give **one** use for each of them. *(4 marks)*

Hydrogen is produced. It is used as a fuel. Chlorine is produced. It is used to make bleach.

### EXAM ALERT!

Remember that the products of electrolysis of brine are used to make other substances. For example, sodium hydroxide is used to **make** soap (rather than saying soap is formed when brine undergoes electrolysis!).

Students have struggled with exam questions similar to this – **be prepared!**

Hydrogen is also used in the manufacture of ammonia and margarine. Chlorine is also useful for making plastics.

### Now try this

Remember that hydrogen ions are $H^+$ and chloride ions are $Cl^-$.

**(target G-E)**
1. Give **one** reason why aluminium is expensive to produce. *(1 mark)*
2. Explain why cryolite is used in the electrolyte during aluminium extraction. *(2 marks)*

**(target D-C)**
3. Two gases are produced during the electrolysis of sodium chloride solution. Explain which gas is produced at each electrode. *(4 marks)*

# Electrolysis products

## At the electrodes

If an electrolyte is an ionic compound dissolved in water, it will contain:
- hydrogen ions from the water ($H^+$)
- positive ions from the ionic compound.
- hydroxide ions from the water ($OH^-$)
- negative ions from the ionic compound.

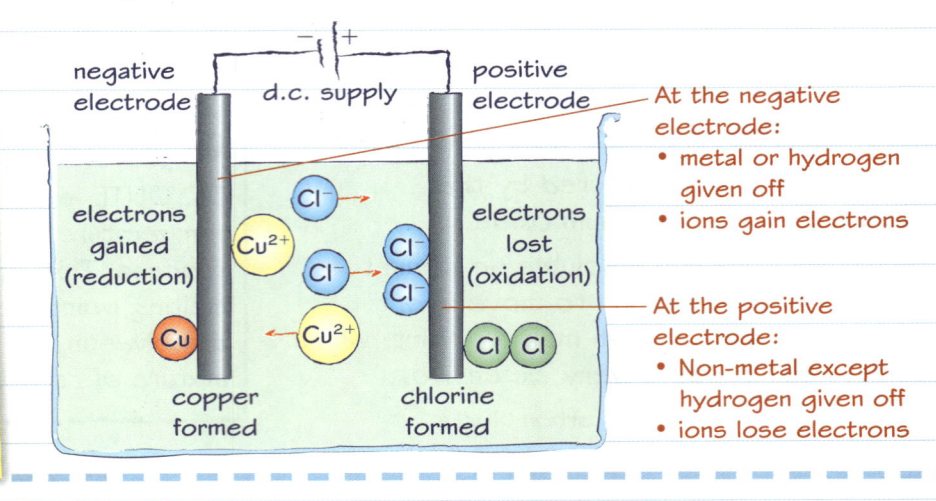

At the negative electrode:
- metal or hydrogen given off
- ions gain electrons

At the positive electrode:
- Non-metal except hydrogen given off
- ions lose electrons

## At the negative electrode

Hydrogen ions will be discharged, producing hydrogen, unless the compound contains ions from a less reactive metal than hydrogen. In that case the metal is produced instead. Copper and silver are below hydrogen on the reactivity series (see page 99).

## At the positive electrode

Hydroxide ions will be discharged, producing oxygen, unless the compound contains halide ions. In that case:
- chlorides produce chlorine
- bromides produce bromine
- iodides produce iodine.

## Worked example

Predict the products formed at each electrode during the electrolysis of the following electrolytes.

**(a) Molten zinc chloride.** (2 marks)

Zinc at the negative electrode and chlorine at the positive electrode.

*Molten zinc chloride only contains zinc ions and chloride ions.*

**(b) Potassium iodide solution.** (2 marks)

Hydrogen at the negative electrode and iodine at the positive electrode.

*Potassium is more reactive than hydrogen, which means that hydrogen is given off at the electrode. Iodide ions are discharged as iodine.*

**(c) Sulfuric acid.** (2 marks)

Hydrogen at the negative electrode and oxygen at the positive electrode.

*Hydrogen ions and hydroxide ions are discharged. Notice that sulfur is not produced.*

Solutions will contain hydrogen ions and hydroxide ions from the water, as well as the ions from the dissolved compound.

## Now try this

1. Sodium chloride solution contains sodium ions and chloride ions. Name **two** other ions it contains, and explain where they come from. (3 marks)

2. Sir Humphry Davy first produced potassium by the electrolysis of molten potassium hydroxide in 1807. Davy's earlier attempts using potassium hydroxide solution did not work. Explain the difference between the results of Davy's two experiments. (4 marks)

Had a look ☐   Nearly there ☐   Nailed it! ☐   **CHEMISTRY**

# Chemistry six mark question 3

There will be one 6 mark question on your exam paper, which will be marked for *quality of written communication* as well as scientific knowledge. This means that you need to apply your scientific knowledge, present your answer in a logical and organised way, and make sure that your spelling, grammar and punctuation are as good as you can make them.

## Worked example

*AQA SKILL: Describe — Page 101*

### Practical work

Most of your practical work is assessed through the ISA, but you do need to be able to apply your knowledge to practical questions on the exam paper as well. There are very few experiments that you have to learn but you do need to know how to prepare salts from different substances.

Sodium chloride is a soluble salt made when hydrochloric acid reacts with sodium hydroxide solution:

hydrochloric acid + sodium hydroxide → sodium chloride + water

Describe how to make crystals of sodium chloride. You should include how you will add the correct amount of hydrochloric acid to neutralise the sodium hydroxide solution, and how you will get the crystals.

sodium chloride crystals formed by evaporating the water

(6 marks)

Use a measuring cylinder to add 25 cm³ of sodium hydroxide solution to a conical flask. Add a few drops of phenolphthalein indicator. Use a burette to add hydrochloric acid to the flask, mixing all the time. Near the end point of the reaction, add the acid drop by drop. Stop adding it when the indicator changes colour, and make a note of the volume added.

Repeat, but this time without the indicator, adding the same volumes of acid and alkali as before. Pour the solution into an evaporating dish and warm using a Bunsen burner to evaporate most of the water. Leave on a windowsill so that the rest of the water evaporates, leaving crystals behind.

> The actual volume is not important, only that you know what it is. Phenolphthalein is a better choice than universal indicator because it changes colour suddenly. The acid could be added from a measuring cylinder or a pipette instead.

> Charcoal could be used to remove the indicator from the mixture, instead of repeating. Filtration would be needed to remove the charcoal. Bigger crystals are made if the water evaporates slowly.

## Now try this

Aluminium oxide is an ionic compound that contains aluminium ions, $Al^{3+}$, and oxide ions, $O^{2-}$. Aluminium is made from purified aluminium oxide using electrolysis. The electrolysis apparatus has carbon electrodes and contains a mixture of molten cryolite and aluminium oxide.

Explain how aluminium and carbon dioxide are formed in this process.  (6 marks)

> Think about what the positive and negative ions do during electrolysis, and the substances they produce when they reach the electrodes. What reaction will make carbon dioxide?

# Resultant forces

The forces acting on an object can change how it moves.

When one object exerts a force on a second object the second object exerts an equal and opposite force on the first object.

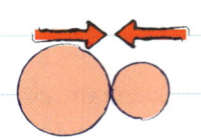

*The arrow shows the direction of the force. The size of the arrow suggests the size of the force.*

## Resultant forces

*Two or more forces acting on an object can be replaced by one force. This is called the resultant force.*

- large force in this direction
- small force in this direction
- resultant force

If two or more forces are acting in the same straight line or are parallel they can be added together to find the RESULTANT force.

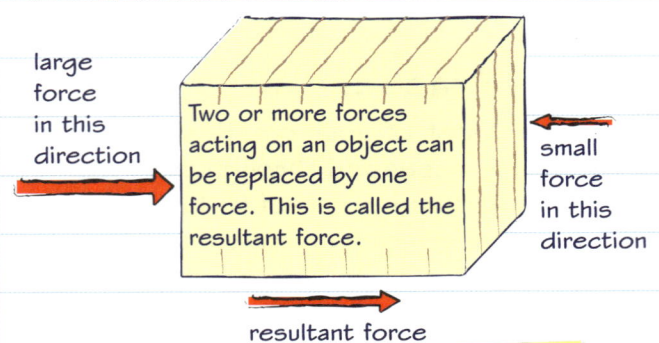

*Forces have direction, so a force of −1 N is in the opposite direction to a force of +1 N.*

### EXAM ALERT!

A common mistake is to think that when the resultant force on an object is zero, the object must be stationary – it may be travelling at constant speed.

Students have struggled with exam questions similar to this – **be prepared!**

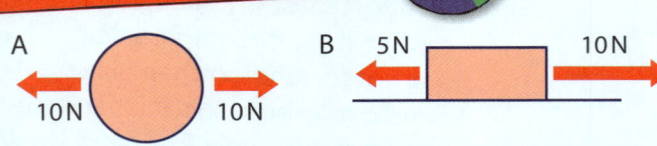

If object B was stationary it will start moving. If it was already moving to the right it will get faster. If it was already moving to the left it would slow down and eventually begin moving to the right.

## Worked example

A: 10 N ← ○ → 10 N

B: 5 N ← □ → 10 N

**(a)** Explain what will happen to the object in diagram A. *(2 marks)*

The object will stay still. This is because it was stationary to start with and the force moving the object to the left is equal to the force moving the object to the right, so the resultant force is zero.

**(b)** Explain what will happen to the object in diagram B. *(2 marks)*

The object will accelerate to the right. This is because the force to the right is bigger than the force to the left, so the resulting force is acting to the right.

## Now try this

1. A ball falls vertically and hits the ground with a force of 12 N. What is the force of the ground on the ball? *(2 marks)*

2. Two men are pushing on the back of a broken down car. One man exerts a force of 80 N and the other exerts a force of 60 N.
   (a) Calculate the resultant force on the car. *(2 marks)*
   (b) Describe what happens to the car. *(2 marks)*

3. A cyclist is cycling along a level road. She exerts a forward force of 25 N forwards. There is air resistance of 15 N and friction forces of 10 N.
   (a) Calculate the resultant force. Show your working. *(2 marks)*
   (b) State what happens to the motion of the bike. *(1 mark)*

Had a look ☐   Nearly there ☐   Nailed it! ☐

**PHYSICS 2.1.2**

# Forces and motion

The ACCELERATION of an object can be calculated if you know its mass and the resultant force acting on it.

The acceleration of an object can be found using the equation:

$a = F/m$

- $a$ is acceleration in metres per second squared, m/s²
- $F$ is the resultant force acting on the object in newtons, N
- $m$ is the mass of the object in kilograms, kg.

The force can be calculated by re-organising the equation to give:

$F = m \times a$

- The acceleration is in the same direction as the force.
- If the resultant force is zero, the acceleration is zero.
- A negative force means that the object is accelerating backwards or is slowing down.

## Worked example (G-E)

**1** A force of 8 N acts on an object of mass 4 kg. Calculate the acceleration of the object. *(2 marks)*

$a = \dfrac{8 \text{ N}}{4 \text{ kg}} = 2 \text{ m/s}^2$

*Make sure you get the units correct.*

**2** A car with a mass of 800 kg has an acceleration of 1.5 m/s². Calculate the resultant force acting on the car. *(2 marks)*

$F = 800 \text{ kg} \times 1.5 \text{ m/s}^2 = 1200 \text{ N}$

## Worked example (D-C)

**1** A basketball player catches a ball of mass 0.6 kg. The acceleration of the ball is −2.4 m/s².

**(a)** Calculate the force on the ball. *(2 marks)*

$F = 0.6 \text{ kg} \times -2.4 \text{ m/s}^2 = -1.44 \text{ N}$

*Make sure you include minus signs in your calculations.*

**(b)** Which of the following describes the effect of the force on the ball? Tick (✓) **one** box. *(1 mark)*

| | |
|---|---|
| The ball is moving backwards. | |
| The ball is slowing down moving forwards. | ✓ |
| The ball is moving faster forwards. | |

## Now try this

**1** (G-E) An object with a mass of 5 kg experiences a force of 20 N.
  **(a)** Calculate the acceleration of the object in the diagram. *(2 marks)*
  **(b)** Describe how the object is moving. *(2 marks)*

**2** (D-C) The *SpaceX Dragon* capsule is used to deliver supplies to the International Space Station. It has a mass of 3200 kg when loaded. It uses thrusters with a force of 400 N to manoeuvre in space. Calculate the acceleration of the Dragon capsule when a thruster is applying its full force. State the units in your answer. *(3 marks)*

**3** (D-C) A cricket ball with a mass of 0.16 kg is hit straight upwards. The ball experiences a force that gives it an acceleration of −10 m/s².
  **(a)** Calculate the force acting on the ball. *(2 marks)*
  **(b)** Explain the motion of the ball. *(2 marks)*

# PHYSICS 2.1.2

Had a look ☐   Nearly there ☐   Nailed it! ☐

# Distance–time graphs

DISTANCE–TIME GRAPHS give information about the motion of an object.

A distance–time graph shows how far an object has travelled from a starting point at various times.

The graph shows the motion of three objects A, B and C.

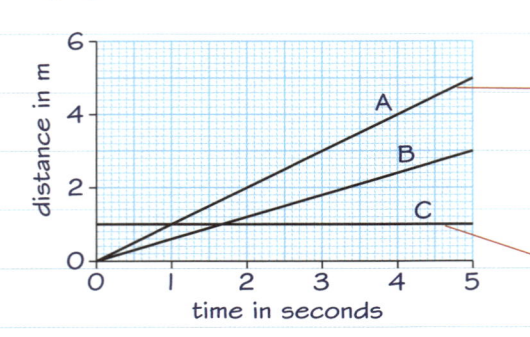

A and B started from the same point but after 5 s A has travelled further than B. The speed of A is greater than B, and this is shown by the gradient of the lines. The steeper the gradient the greater the speed.

The distance of object C from the starting point does not change, so it must be stationary. A horizontal line represents a speed of 0 m/s.

## Worked example (target G-E)

**1** The graphs show the distance travelled by two vehicles at various times. The statements describe how they move. Draw a line from each graph to the description of the motion. **(2 marks)**

**Graphs** — **Descriptions**
- (horizontal line graph) → stationary
- (rising line graph) → moving forwards at constant speed
- moving backwards at a constant speed

## Worked example (target D-C)

**1** Explain why a car travelling around a roundabout may be travelling at a steady speed, but its velocity is changing. **(2 marks)**

If it is moving in a circle its direction is changing so the velocity must be changing.

> Velocity is the speed of an object in a given direction. If an object changes direction, its velocity changes even if its speed remains constant.

## Now try this (target G-E)

**1 (a)** Draw a distance–time graph for the data given in the table below. Label this line A. **(4 marks)**

| Time in s | Distance travelled by vehicle A in m |
|---|---|
| 0 | 0 |
| 1 | 4 |
| 2 | 8 |
| 3 | 12 |
| 4 | 16 |

**(b)** Add a second line to your graph, labelled line B, for a vehicle that starts from the same point as A but with a higher speed. **(2 marks)**

**(c)** Vehicle C is 5 m from where vehicle A started. Vehicle C is stationary. Draw a line labelled C to show this. **(2 marks)**

AQA SKILL Draw — Page 101

Had a look ☐   Nearly there ☐   Nailed it! ☐

**PHYSICS 2.1.2**

# Acceleration and velocity

Acceleration is the rate of change of velocity (or speed in a straight line).

Acceleration can be calculated using the equation:

$$a = \frac{v - u}{t}$$

- $a$ is acceleration in metres per second squared, m/s²
- $u$ is the initial velocity in metres per second, m/s   *Initial means 'at the start'.*
- $v$ is the final velocity in metres per second, m/s
- $t$ is the time taken in seconds, s, for the change in velocity to happen.

## Velocity–time graphs

Velocity–time graphs show how the velocity of an object changes.

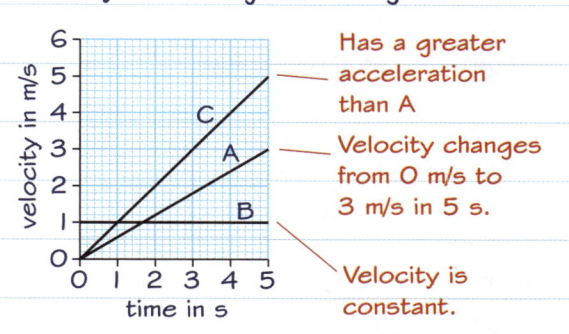

- C — Has a greater acceleration than A
- A — Velocity changes from 0 m/s to 3 m/s in 5 s.
- B — Velocity is constant.

## EXAM ALERT!

Make sure that you know what sort of graph you are dealing with, a distance–time graph or a velocity–time graph. The gradients of the two types of graph represent different quantities.

Students have struggled with exam questions similar to this – **be prepared!**

## Worked example  *target D-C*

**1** A train travelling at 30 m/s on a straight track increases its speed to 50 m/s in 8 s. Calculate the acceleration of the train.
*(2 marks)*

$u$ = 30 m/s, $v$ = 50 m/s, $t$ = 8 s

$$a = \frac{50 \text{ m/s} - 30 \text{ m/s}}{8 \text{ s}} = 20/8 = 2.5 \text{ m/s}^2$$

*The steeper the gradient the greater the acceleration*

## Now try this

**target G-E**

**1** The graph shows how the velocity of an object changes with time.

Circle the correct answer in the sentences below to complete the statements.

**(a)** Between 0 and 4 seconds the object is

| moving at a constant speed   accelerating   stationary |.
*(1 mark)*

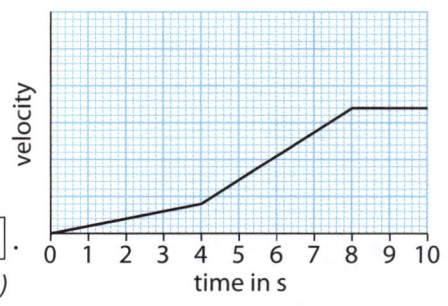

**(b)** Between 4 and 8 seconds the object

| has a larger acceleration   has a smaller acceleration   is stationary |.
*(1 mark)*

**(c)** After 8 seconds the object is

| stationary   accelerating   moving at a constant velocity |.
*(1 mark)*

**target D-C**

**2** An aircraft is stationary at the end of the runway. It starts moving and after 40 s reaches its take-off speed of 80 m/s. Calculate the acceleration of the aircraft.
*(2 marks)*

# Forces and braking

**PHYSICS 2.1.3** — Had a look ☐ Nearly there ☐ Nailed it! ☐

How long it takes a vehicle to stop depends on lots of different factors, including braking force.

## Resistive forces

A lorry is travelling at a steady speed. The **resistive forces** (R) are equal and opposite to the driving force (F). The main resistive force is **air resistance**. It is sometimes called 'drag'.

## Stopping distance

Stopping distance is the distance a vehicle travels from the moment the driver sees something happen on the road ahead to when the vehicle is stationary.

**stopping distance = thinking distance + braking distance**

- Thinking distance is the distance travelled in the time it takes for the driver to react. The greater the speed of a vehicle, the further it will travel while the driver is reacting.
- Braking distance is the distance travelled while the brakes are applying a force to slow the vehicle.

## Braking force and distance

The greater the speed of the vehicle the greater the braking force needed to stop in a particular distance. For a constant braking force the braking distance increases with speed.

The brakes produce a frictional force between the brake and wheel. The kinetic energy of the vehicle is reduced. Energy is transferred to the brakes and the temperature of the brakes increases.

Braking distance is increased by ice or water on the road, and by worn brakes or tyres.

Thinking distance is also increased when a driver is tired, or has taken drugs, or is distracted by a mobile phone or by conversation.

## Worked example (target D-C)

Look at the data in the table below.

| Speed in mph | Thinking distance in m | |
|---|---|---|
| | Without alcohol | With alcohol |
| 20 | 6 | 10 |
| 30 | 9 | 15 |
| 40 | 12 | 20 |

**(a)** State the effect that drinking alcohol has on thinking distance. *(1 mark)*

Alcohol increases the time taken for the driver to react. This means that thinking distance increases.

**(b)** Describe the effect that driving after drinking alcohol has on stopping distances. *(2 marks)*

Alcohol increases thinking distance which means that the overall stopping distance will increase.

## Now try this

1. (target G-E) A child steps into a road 25 m in front of a moving car. The car travels 9 m while the driver reacts and a further 14 m while the brakes bring it to a standstill. Show that the car will not hit the child. *(3 marks)*

2. (target D-C) Explain what happens to the kinetic energy a cyclist has when the cyclist brakes and stops moving. *(2 marks)*

3. Suggest **two** reasons why a Formula 1 racing car driven by a top driver can stop in a shorter distance than someone driving their car home after a day's work. Both cars are travelling at the same speed. *(2 marks)*

Had a look ☐  Nearly there ☐  Nailed it! ☐

**PHYSICS 2.1.4**

# Falling objects

The resultant force acting on a falling object depends on its WEIGHT and the AIR RESISTANCE.

## Weight and gravity

The weight of an object is the force exerted on it by gravity.

$W = m \times g$

- $W$ is the weight of the object in newtons, N
- $m$ is the mass of the object in kilograms, kg
- $g$ is the gravitational field strength in newtons per kilogram, N/kg

## Falling and terminal velocity

An object starts to fall through a fluid such as water. The weight of the object makes it accelerate. Weight always acts downwards. The resistance of the fluid causes an upward force.

As the falling object accelerates the resistance forces increase.

When the resultant force is zero the object falls at a constant velocity called TERMINAL VELOCITY

## Worked example (G–E)

**1** A bag of sugar has a mass of 0.5 kg.

**(a)** Calculate the weight of the sugar. The gravitational field strength of the Earth is 10 N/kg. *(2 marks)*

$W = 0.5 \text{ kg} \times 10 \text{ N/kg} = 5 \text{ N}$

**(b)** Explain why the same bag of sugar will have a lower weight on the Moon. The gravitational field strength of the Moon is 1.7 N/kg. *(2 marks)*

The weight of the bag of sugar is lower on the Moon because the gravitational field strength of the Moon is lower than that of the Earth.

## Worked example (D–C)

A skydiver opens a parachute at terminal velocity. Fill in the correct word to complete each sentence. *(4 marks)*

When the parachute opens the frictional force of the air on the skydiver becomes <u>larger</u> because the area has suddenly increased. There is a resultant force acting <u>upwards</u> and the skydiver's velocity <u>decreases</u>.

The frictional force reduces until the resultant force is <u>zero</u> and the skydiver falls at a terminal velocity, which is <u>smaller</u> without the parachute.

## Now try this

**1** An adult woman has a mass of 62 kg. Calculate the woman's weight and state the unit. Gravitational field strength = 10 N/kg. *(3 marks)* **(G–E)**

**2** A skydiver jumps from a capsule hanging from a balloon 23 km above the surface of the Earth. Tick (✓) **one** box in each row to show whether weight or air resistance are greater at different stages of the fall. *(4 marks)* **(D–C)**

| Stage of the fall | Weight greater than resistance | Weight equals resistance | Resistance greater than weight |
|---|---|---|---|
| He steps out of the capsule. | | | |
| He is falling at a constant, high velocity. | | | |
| He opens his parachute. | | | |
| He is falling at a constant, low velocity of a few m/s. | | | |

# Forces and terminal velocity

Velocity–time graphs show the changing forces on a falling object.

The graph shows the stages in the fall of a skydiver.

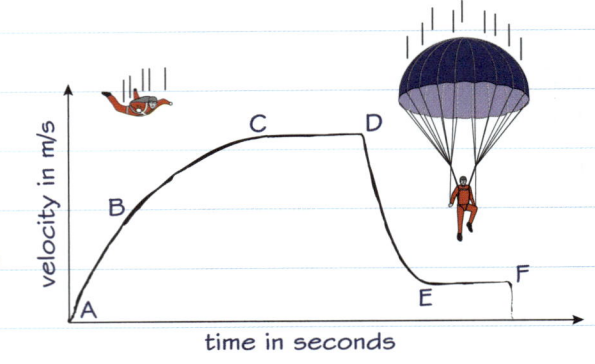

1. **AB:** The force of gravity pulls the skydiver downwards. Air resistance is small so the resultant force is large. The skydiver accelerates.
2. **BC:** As the velocity of the skydiver increases the air resistance increases. Weight remains constant. The resultant force gets smaller and the acceleration decreases.
3. **CD:** The air resistance is equal and opposite to the weight of the skydiver. The resultant force is zero so acceleration is zero. The skydiver has reached terminal velocity.
4. **DE:** The skydiver opens the parachute. The larger surface area increases the air resistance so that it is bigger than the weight. The resultant force is upwards. This means the acceleration downwards is negative. The skydiver's velocity reduces. As the velocity reduces, the air resistance decreases until it is again equal to the weight
5. **EF:** The skydiver falls to the ground at a new lower terminal velocity and hits the ground at F and stops.

## Worked example

A diver wears weights around her waist to make her sink in the sea. Her total weight is 80 N.

(a) During the dive she falls through the water at a constant velocity. Which of the following will be the upwards force that the water exerts on the diver? Put a ring around the correct answer. *(1 mark)*

Less than 80 N   **(80 N)**   more than 80 N

The diver reaches terminal velocity when the resistive force is equal to the diver's weight.

(b) Sketch a velocity–time graph showing what happens to the diver as she falls through the water. Label the stages of your graph. *(4 marks)*

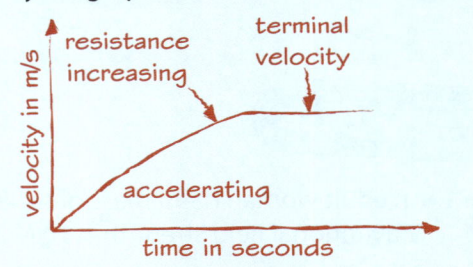

## Now try this

1. Look at the velocity–time graph for a skydiver at the top of this page. Give the letters corresponding to the stage(s) where:
   (a) upwards and downwards forces are equal *(1 mark)*
   (b) the weight of the skydiver is greater than the air resistance. *(1 mark)*
   (c) the resultant downwards force is negative. *(1 mark)*

2. A parachutist jumps off a cliff with the parachute already open. The parachutist reaches a terminal velocity of 20 m/s after 3 s. Sketch a velocity–time graph of the first 6 s of the fall. *(3 marks)*

Had a look ☐   Nearly there ☐   Nailed it! ☐    PHYSICS 2.1.5

# Elasticity

## Forces on an object

Forces can change the shape of objects and sometimes energy can be stored. An object is elastic if it recovers its original shape when the force is removed. The stored elastic potential energy is transferred to the surroundings and increases the temperature.

A force acting on an object may cause it to change shape. This includes stretching, compressing, bending or twisting the object into a new shape.

When a force moves a part of the object it does work. Doing work transfers energy.

If the object is elastic then some of this transferred energy is stored as elastic potential energy.

### Forces and extension

The extension is the change in length of the object when it is stretched. The extension of an elastic object is directly proportional to the stretching force applied to it. This is shown in the equation:
$F = k \times e$
- $F$ is the applied force in newtons, N
- $k$ is the spring constant for the object in newtons per metre, N/m
- $e$ is the extension of the object in metres, m

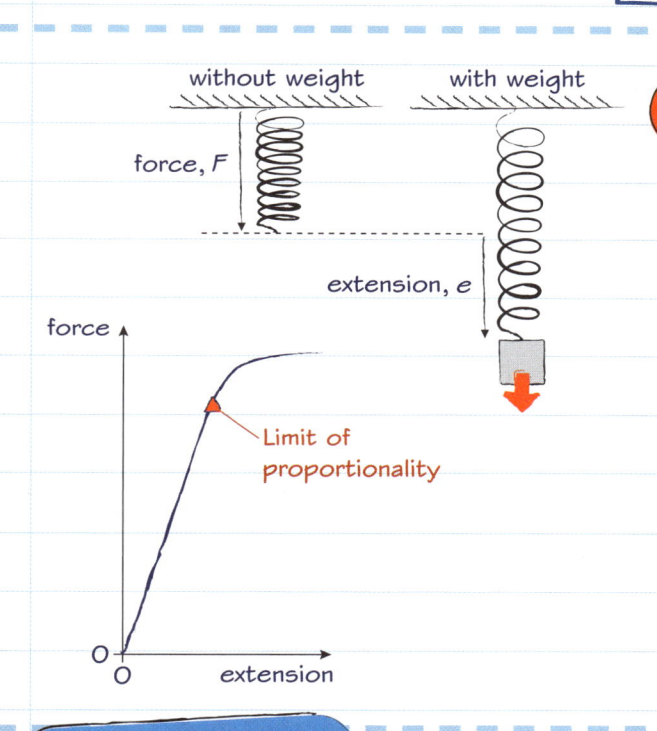

### Worked example (target D-C)

A spring has a spring constant of 40 N/m. The spring is 12 cm long. When a weight is hung from the spring its length increases to 17 cm. Calculate the weight hung from the spring. *(4 marks)*

The extension of the spring
= 17 cm − 12 cm = 5 cm
5 cm is 0.05 m
$F = 40 \text{ N/m} \times 0.05 \text{ m} = 2 \text{ N}$

The equation only applies up to a certain extension. This is called the **limit of proportionality**. For greater forces the equation does not apply.

## Now try this

**1** Complete the sentences.

(target G-E)

(a) An elastic object stores elastic potential energy when it is _____ by a force. *(1 mark)*

(b) Elastic potential energy is transferred from an elastic object when it _____. *(1 mark)*

(c) The extension of a spring increases when the force applied to it _____. *(1 mark)*

**2** The rope used in a bungee jump is 50 m long. When a man jumps with the bungee attached he ends up hanging 54 m below his starting point. The spring constant of the bungee is 230 N/m. Calculate the weight of the man. *(3 marks)*

(target D-C)

**PHYSICS 2.2.1** — Had a look ☐   Nearly there ☐   Nailed it! ☐

# Forces and energy

Force, work, energy and power are all quantities related to moving objects.

## Work

WORK is done when a force causes an object to move through a distance.

Energy is transferred from one form to another when work is done.

*accelerating* — The thrust of a vehicle does work in transferring the energy stored in the fuel into kinetic energy. The velocity of the vehicle increases.

*braking* — A resistive force does work in transferring kinetic energy of a moving object to increase the temperature of the object and surroundings. The object slows down.

The work done by a force is given by the equation:

work = force × distance

$W = F \times d$

W is the work done in joules, J

F is the force acting on the object in newtons, N

d is the distance moved by the object while the force is acting, in metres, m. The distance must be measured in the same direction as the force is acting.

> The amount of energy transferred is equal to the amount of work done.

### Power

Power is the amount of work done or energy transferred in a given time.

power = energy/time

$P = E/t$

- P is power in watts, W
- E is the energy transferred or work done in joules, J
- t is the time taken in seconds, s

A power of 1 watt is 1 joule per second.

---

## Worked example  *target D-C*

**1** A rocket taking off from a launch pad transfers 250 000 000 J of energy in the 4 s it takes to get to the top of the launch tower.

**(a)** What is meant by the power of the rocket? *(2 marks)*

Power is the amount of work done or energy transferred in a given time.

**(b)** Calculate the power of the rocket. *(2 marks)*

$$P = \frac{250\,000\,000 \text{ J}}{4 \text{ s}} = 62\,500\,000 \text{ W}$$

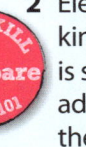

**2** Electric cars use regenerative braking to transfer kinetic energy into electrical energy, which is stored the vehicle's batteries. Explain the advantage of this type of braking compared with the brakes used in older vehicles. *(3 marks)*

*(AQA SKILL — Compare — Page 101)*

In older vehicles the energy transferred when braking is wasted by raising the temperature of the surroundings. With regenerative braking the energy stored can be used again to increase the kinetic energy of the vehicle. It reduces the amount of wasted or dissipated energy.

---

## Now try this

*target G-E*

**1** A cyclist travelling along a road applies the brakes with a force of 80 N. The bike stops in a distance of 4 m.

**(a)** Calculate the energy transferred to the brakes. *(3 marks)*

**(b)** It takes 2 s for the cyclist to stop. Calculate the power used by the brakes. *(2 marks)*

*target D-C*

**2** A meteorite entering the atmosphere from space becomes extremely hot and evaporates before it hits the ground. Explain why this happens. *(2 marks)*

Had a look ☐  Nearly there ☐  Nailed it! ☐

**PHYSICS 2.2.1**

# KE and GPE

Kinetic energy (KE) and gravitational potential energy (GPE) are two forms of energy

GRAVITATIONAL POTENTIAL ENERGY is the energy an object has because of its position in a gravitational field.

Lifting an object does work against the gravitational force (weight). As a result, the object gains gravitational potential energy.

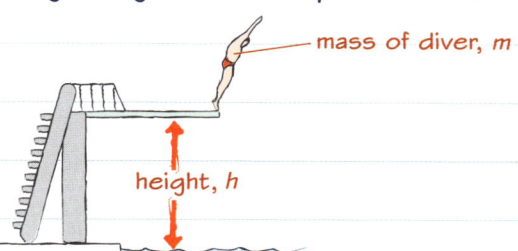

— mass of diver, $m$
— height, $h$

Gravitational potential energy
= mass × gravitational field strength × height difference
$$E_p = m \times g \times h$$

- $E_p$ is gravitational potential energy in joules, J
- $m$ is the mass of the object in kilograms, kg
- $g$ is the gravitational field strength in newtons/kilogram, N/kg
- $h$ is the height above a given level in metres, m

KINETIC ENERGY is the energy an object has when it is moving. It depends on the mass and speed of the object.

kinetic energy = $\frac{1}{2}$ × mass × velocity$^2$
$$E_k = \frac{1}{2} \times m \times v^2$$

- $E_k$ is kinetic energy in joules, J
- $m$ is the mass of the object in kilograms, kg
- $v$ is the speed of the object in metres per second, m/s

> The direction the object moves is not important in calculating kinetic energy.

### EXAM ALERT!

Don't forget that $v^2$ means speed-squared, or $v \times v$.

Students have struggled with this topic in recent exams – **be prepared!**

> When an object falls its gravitational potential energy is transferred into kinetic energy.

## Worked example  (D-C)

**AQA SKILL Evaluate  Page 101**

Modern cars are fitted with seat belts, air bags and crumple zones to protect the occupants in a crash. About 90% of drivers and passengers in the UK wear seat belts. About 50% of the people killed in car accidents are found to have not been wearing seat belts. Evaluate the benefits of wearing seat belts.
*(2 marks)*

Only a few people do not wear seat belts, but they form a large fraction of the number of deaths. This suggests that not wearing seat belts is more likely to lead to death in an accident than wearing a seat belt. Therefore, wearing a seat belt makes you safer when travelling in a car.

> Work is done in changing the shape of the crumple zones, in stretching the seat belts and in compressing the air bag. This work transfers the kinetic energy of the car and the occupants into raising the temperature and other forms of energy. This means less of the energy is transferred to the occupants, so they are less likely to be injured.

## Now try this

**(G-E)** 1  A man with a mass of 70 kg climbs stairs that are 3 m high. Calculate the gravitational potential energy he gains. The Earth's gravitational field strength is 10 N/kg. *(2 marks)*

**(D-C)** 2  Felix Baumgartner fell from the edge of space and reached a maximum speed of 373 m/s. If his total mass was 200 kg what was his maximum kinetic energy? *(2 marks)*

**PHYSICS 2.2.2** — Had a look ☐   Nearly there ☐   Nailed it! ☐

# Momentum

The MOMENTUM of an object depends on both its mass and its velocity.

momentum = mass × velocity
$p = m \times v$

- $p$ is the momentum of an object in kilogram metres per second, kg m/s
- $m$ is the mass of the object in kilograms, kg
- $v$ is the velocity of the object in metres per second, m/s

*Like velocity, momentum has a specified direction.*

*A closed system is one in which no objects or energy are added or taken away.*

## Conservation of momentum

In a closed system, the total momentum of all the objects before an event (such as a collision or explosion) is the same as the total momentum after the collision.

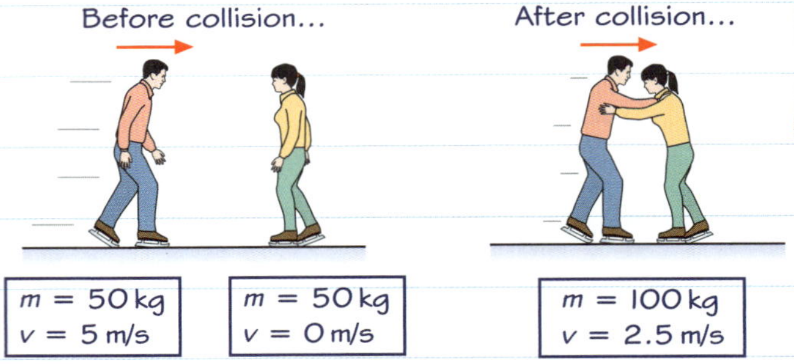

Before collision...
| $m = 50$ kg | $m = 50$ kg |
| $v = 5$ m/s | $v = 0$ m/s |

Total momentum
= 50 kg × 5 m/s + 50 kg × 0 m/s
= 250 kg m/s

After collision...
$m = 100$ kg
$v = 2.5$ m/s

Total momentum
= 100 kg × 2.5 m/s
= 250 kg m/s

---

### Worked example (target D-C)

**1** A rocket sits on the launch pad.

**(a)** The rocket fires and 50 kg of gases leave the rocket with a velocity of 150 m/s downwards. Calculate the momentum of the gases. *(2 marks)*

$p = 50 \text{ kg} \times 150 \text{ m/s} = 7500 \text{ kg m/s}$

**(b)** Calculate the momentum of the rocket as it moves upwards. *(2 marks)*

$p_{gases} + p_{rocket} = 0$,
therefore $p_{rocket} = -p_{gases} = -7500$ kg m/s

*The momentum of the rocket on the launch pad is zero. The total momentum of the rocket and the gases stays zero.*

**(c)** Explain why the rocket moves upwards. *(2 marks)*

The rocket moves in the opposite direction to the gases because momentum is conserved.

**2** Explain why crumple zones on a car reduce injuries to the driver in a crash. *(2 marks)*

The work done in crushing the crumple zone reduces the velocity of the vehicle. This means that if the driver is wearing a seat belt, he has a smaller momentum as he hits the steering wheel.

---

### Now try this

**target G-E**

**1** A car and a truck are travelling at the same speed. Explain which has the larger momentum. *(2 marks)*

**target D-C**

**2** A model railway carriage with a mass of 0.2 kg is moving at 0.8 m/s towards a stationary carriage with the same mass.

**(a)** Calculate the total momentum of the two railway carriages. *(3 marks)*

The first carriage collides with the second and they move off together.

**(b)** Explain why the total momentum remains the same after the collision. *(2 marks)*

**(c)** Explain the direction the carriages move after the collision. *(2 marks)*

Had a look ☐  Nearly there ☐  Nailed it! ☐   **PHYSICS**

# Physics six mark question 1

There will be one 6 mark question on your exam paper, which will be marked for *quality of written communication* as well as scientific knowledge. This means that you need to apply your scientific knowledge, present your answer in a logical and organised way, and make sure that your spelling, grammar and punctuation are as good as you can make them.

## Worked example

When a skydiver falls through the air he experiences forces before and after he opens his parachute.

Explain why the forces change and the effect the forces have on the skydiver's velocity.

(6 marks)

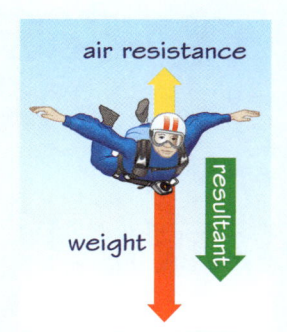

An object such as a skydiver falling through the air experiences the resultant force of his weight, which acts downwards, and air resistance, which acts upwards. The size of the air resistance depends on his velocity.

At first his velocity is low, so air resistance is low. This makes the resultant force large in a downwards direction, so his velocity increases. The air resistance increases as his velocity increases until it balances his weight and the resultant becomes zero. He falls at a constant velocity called the terminal velocity.

When he opens the parachute there is a large increase in air resistance because the area of the parachute in contact with the air is much greater and the resultant force is upwards so the skydiver slows down. The air resistance decreases until it is again balanced by the weight. The resultant is zero and he falls at a lower terminal velocity.

### Explain

The question uses the command 'explain'. This means you should state the changes that take place in the skydiver's fall and say why they happen.

The question suggests that there are two stages in the fall — before and after the parachute opens. Make sure that you give an answer for both stages.

Remember that:

resultant force (down) = weight − air resistance

The resultant force affects the acceleration — that is, the rate of change in velocity.

This is a good answer because it details all the changes that take place in the skydiver's fall and explains the changes in velocity that occur.

## Now try this

A driver of a vehicle observes an obstacle in the road some distance in front of her. Explain how various factors affect the stopping distance of the vehicle and determine whether the vehicle will stop before hitting the obstacle.

(6 marks)

**PHYSICS 2.3.1** | Had a look ☐ | Nearly there ☐ | Nailed it! ☐

# Static electricity

Some materials can be given a charge of static electricity.

Some materials become ELECTRICALLY CHARGED when rubbed by another material. These charges are fixed or STATIC because the materials used are INSULATORS. The electrons cannot travel through the materials.

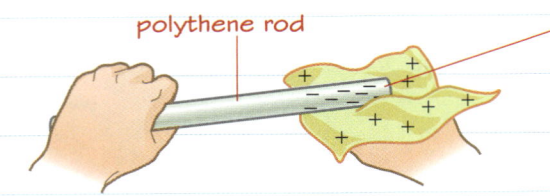

*polythene rod*

Negatively charged ELECTRONS from one material (the cloth) are rubbed onto the other material (the polythene rod). The two materials gain equal and opposite charges.

The material that gains electrons becomes NEGATIVELY CHARGED. The material that loses electrons becomes POSITIVELY CHARGED.

Electrons move around the nucleus of atoms, so it is always the electrons that are transferred. Protons are never transferred.

Silk, wool, nylon and polythene are examples of insulators.

Electrical charges can move easily through conducting materials such as metals.

## Worked example (target G-E)

Describe what happens when two electrically charged objects are brought close together.
*(3 marks)*

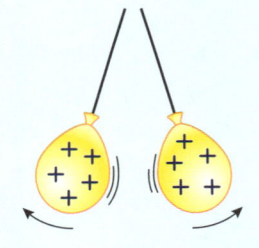

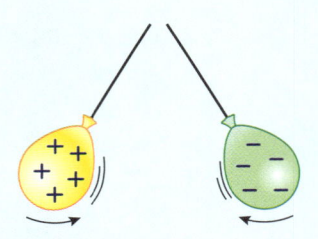

The charged objects exert a force on each other. If the two objects have the same type of electrical charge they repel each other. If they have different types of electrical charge they attract each other.

## Now try this

**1** (target G-E) A student rubs two polythene rods with a woollen cloth. Which of the following will not happen? Tick (✓) **one** box. *(1 mark)*

| | |
|---|---|
| The rods will pick up small pieces of paper. | |
| The rods will attract the cloth. | |
| The rods will be attracted to each other. | |

**2** (target D-C) When clothes made of different materials are dried together in a tumble dryer they often cling together. Explain why this happens. *(3 marks)*

Had a look ☐   Nearly there ☐   Nailed it! ☐

**PHYSICS 2.3.2**

# Current and potential difference

When electric charges move they produce a CURRENT and a POTENTIAL DIFFERENCE.

## Worked example (target G-E)

**(a)** What is an electric current? *(1 mark)*

An electric current is a flow of electrical charge.

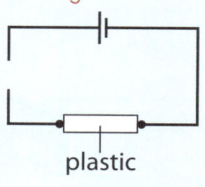

An electric current will only flow through a conductor such as a metal.

(circuit diagram labelled "plastic")

**(b)** Give **two** reasons why there is no current in this circuit. *(2 marks)*

There is a break in the circuit and a part of the circuit is an insulator.

**(c)** In an electric circuit 10 C of electric charge pass through the cell in 4 s. Calculate the electrical current in the circuit. *(2 marks)*

I = 10 C / 4 s = 2.5 A

When an electric charge flows it does work and energy is transferred. The potential difference is the amount of energy transferred by each coulomb of electric charge between two points.

$$\text{potential difference} = \frac{\text{work done}}{\text{charge}}$$

$$V = \frac{W}{Q}$$

- $V$ is the potential difference in volts, V
- $W$ is the work done in joules, J
- $Q$ is the electric charge in coulombs, C

### EXAM ALERT!

'Voltage' means the same as potential difference but it will not be used in exam questions. Try to use potential difference in your answers.

Students have struggled with exam questions similar to this – **be prepared!**

The size of the electric current is the rate of the flow of electric charge. A current of 1 amp means that 1 coulomb of charge passes a point every second.

A potential difference of 1 volt means that 1 J of work is done by each coulomb of charge.

current = charge/time

$$I = \frac{Q}{t}$$

- $I$ is the electric current in amperes, A
- $Q$ is the amount of electric charge in coulombs, C
- $t$ is the time in seconds, s.

## Now try this

**1** (target G-E) Match the quantities and their units. *(4 marks)*

| Quantities | Units |
|---|---|
| work done | volts |
| electric current | coulombs |
| electric charge | watts |
| potential difference | joules |
|  | amperes |

**2** (target D-C) An electric hand warmer transfers 90 J of electrical energy in 5 s. 12 coulombs of electric charge flow through it. Calculate:

(a) the potential difference in the heater circuit *(2 marks)*

(b) the current that flows through it. *(2 marks)*

**PHYSICS 2.3.2** | Had a look ☐ | Nearly there ☐ | Nailed it! ☐

# Circuit diagrams

Circuit diagrams use standard symbols for components.

## Circuit diagram symbols

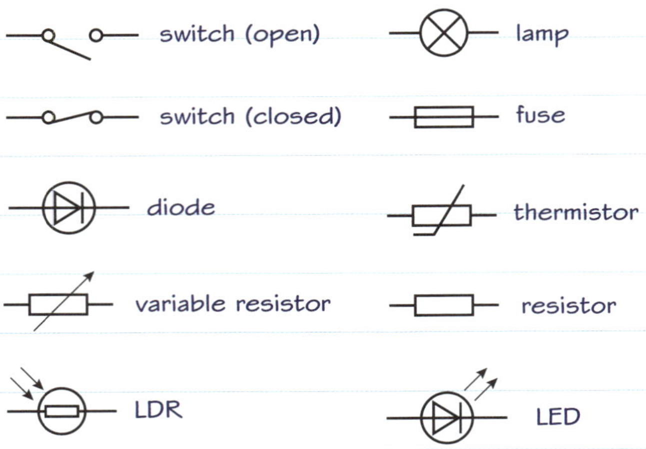

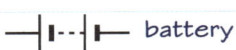

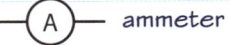

- switch (open)
- lamp
- cell
- voltmeter
- switch (closed)
- fuse
- battery
- ammeter
- diode
- thermistor
- variable resistor
- resistor
- LDR
- LED

### EXAM ALERT!

You need to remember the symbols for each of the components shown here, and you may be asked to draw them.

Students have struggled with this topic in recent exams – **be prepared!**

## Worked example (target G-E)

**1** Draw a circuit to show how a lamp can be made to glow. The circuit needs a source of electrical energy and should be operated by a switch. *(3 marks)*

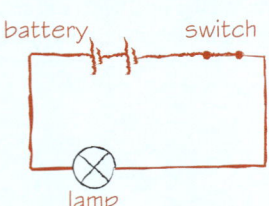

[Circuit diagram showing battery, switch, and lamp in a loop]

Every circuit needs a source of electrical energy. Usually this is shown as a cell or battery.

For charge to flow there must not be any gaps in the circuit.

**2** Match the symbols shown below to their name and function in a circuit. *(3 marks)*

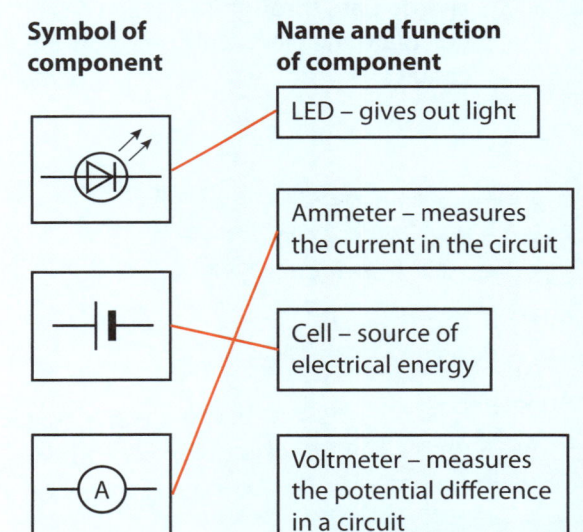

| Symbol of component | Name and function of component |
|---|---|
| LED symbol | LED – gives out light |
| | Ammeter – measures the current in the circuit |
| Cell symbol | Cell – source of electrical energy |
| Ammeter (A) symbol | Voltmeter – measures the potential difference in a circuit |

## Now try this

**(target G-E)**

**1** Look at the three circuit diagrams.

(a) Give the letter of the circuit in which current will flow. *(1 mark)*

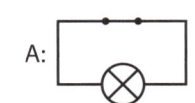

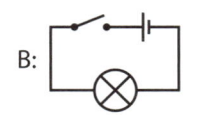

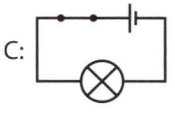

(b) Give a reason why a current flows in this circuit and not in the others. *(2 marks)*

A: [circuit with lamp] B: [circuit with switch, lamp, cell] C: [circuit with lamp, cell]

**(target D-C)**

**2** A student sets up a circuit in which a thermistor, LED, battery and switch are connected together. Draw a circuit diagram for the circuit. *(5 marks)*

Had a look ☐   Nearly there ☐   Nailed it! ☐

**PHYSICS 2.3.2**

# Resistors

A resistor is an electrical component that reduces the current in a circuit.

## Current and potential difference

A current–potential difference graph shows how the current through a component varies as the potential difference across it is changed.

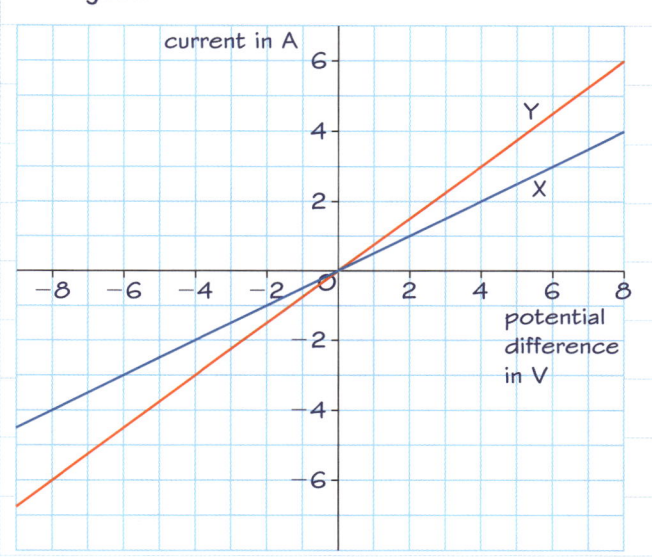

The current through X is lower than Y for the same potential difference. X has the higher **resistance**.

The current–potential difference graph for a resistor at a constant temperature is a straight line through the origin. This shows that the current is directly proportional to the potential difference.

## Worked example  target D-C

A thin length of steel wire has a resistance of 24 Ω. A current of 0.25 A flows through the wire. Calculate the potential difference across the wire.  *(2 marks)*

$$V = 0.25\text{ A} \times 24\text{ Ω} = 6\text{ V}$$

The potential difference across a component depends on the current and the resistance:

potential difference = current × resistance

$$V = I \times R$$

- $V$ is the potential difference in volts, V
- $I$ is the current in amperes, A
- $R$ is the resistance in ohms, Ω.

## Resistance and current

Resistance can be found by measuring current and potential difference. We can rearrange the equation to give:

Resistance = potential difference/current

$$R = V/I$$

We can also rearrange the equation to find the current:

Current = potential difference/resistance

$$I = V/R$$

## Now try this

**target G-E**

1. Look at the current–potential difference graph for resistor X shown above.
   (a) What is the current when the potential difference is 6 V?  *(1 mark)*
   (b) What is the potential difference when the current is −1.5 A?  *(2 marks)*

**target D-C**

2. A student measures the current through two resistors P and Q using the same cell in both circuits. The current through resistor P is 0.5 A and through resistor Q it is 0.25 A. The temperature of the two resistors is the same.
   (a) State what this tells you about the two resistors.  *(2 marks)*
   (b) The resistance of resistor P is 6 Ω. Calculate the potential difference across resistor P and give the unit.  *(2 marks)*

# Series and parallel

The arrangement of components in an electric circuit affects the current and potential difference.

## Series circuits

- In a series circuit the same current flows through all the components.
- The potential difference of cells arranged in series is the sum of the potential difference of each cell. This is only true if the cells are set up the same way round so that the +terminal of one cell is connected to the −terminal of the next.
- The total resistance in a series circuit is the sum of the resistances of each of the components.

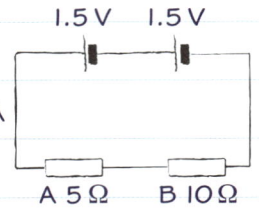

## Parallel circuits

- In a parallel circuit the current divides to pass through the different parts of the circuit.
- The potential difference across each component is the same.

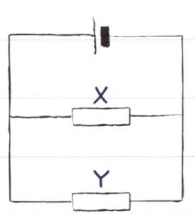

The lights on the tree are in series. If one bulb breaks none of the lights will work.

## Worked example

**1 (a)** Calculate the potential difference in the series circuit above across:

(i) resistor A. *(2 marks)*

$V = 0.2\,A \times 5\,\Omega = 1\,V$

(ii) resistor B. *(2 marks)*

$V = 0.2\,A \times 10\,\Omega = 2\,V$

**(b)** Calculate the total potential difference across both resistors. *(2 marks)*

$V = 1\,V + 2\,V = 3\,V$

The total potential difference supplied by the cells to the circuit is 3 V. This is shared between the resistors in the circuit.

**2** In the parallel circuit above both resistors have a resistance of 8 Ω. The current through each resistor is 0.25 A.

**(a)** Calculate the total current supplied to the circuit by the cell. *(2 marks)*

total current = 0.25 A + 0.25 A = 0.5 A

**(b)** Calculate the potential difference across resistor Y. *(2 marks)*

potential difference = 0.25 A × 8 V = 2 V

The total current is the sum of the currents through each component in a parallel circuit.

## Now try this

You have to know the component symbols given on page 78.

**1** Sketch the circuits described below.

(a) A cell is in series with a light-dependent resistor (LDR) and a resistor. *(2 marks)*

(b) A cell, a diode and a fuse are in parallel with each other. *(2 marks)*

**2** The instructions say that an LED requires a potential difference of 9 V but you only have cells with a potential difference of 1.5 V available. Show an arrangement of cells that would make the LED work. *(2 marks)*

**3** When two lamps are arranged in series they both go out when one breaks. The unbroken one stays on when they are arranged in parallel. Explain this observation. *(3 marks)*

Had a look ☐    Nearly there ☐    Nailed it! ☐    **PHYSICS 2.3.2**

# Variable resistance

The current through some components varies in different ways.

## Filament bulbs

When the potential difference across a filament bulb increases, the temperature of the filament rises. This makes its resistance increase.

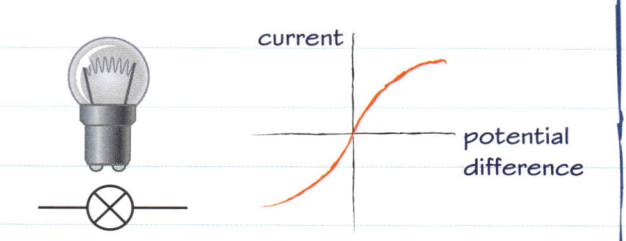

At high potential difference the current through the bulb increases less for each equal increase in potential difference.

## Diodes and LEDs

A current can only flow through a diode in one direction. The resistance of the diode is very high in the reverse direction.

A light-emitting diode (LED) will only give out light when the current flows in the forward direction above a small threshold value.

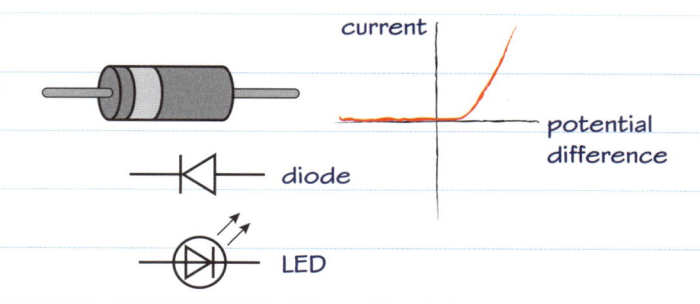

## LDR

The resistance of a light-dependent resistor (LDR) falls as the intensity of light falling on it increases. This means that an LDR allows more current to flow in the light compared to in the dark.

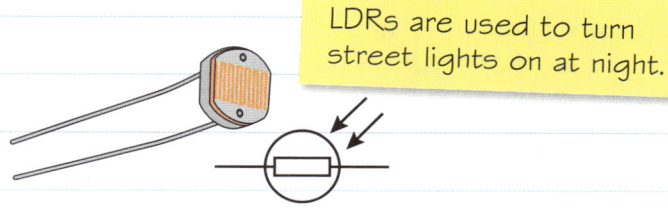

LDRs are used to turn street lights on at night.

## Thermistor

The resistance of a thermistor decreases as the temperature rises. This means that the current through a thermistor rises as the temperature rises.

Thermistors are used in thermostats that control the temperature of appliances such as ovens.

## Now try this

**1** Look at the circuit.

In the circuit shown the LED is only lit when light falls on the circuit. Which of the following is the reason for this? Tick (✓) **one** box.  *(1 mark)*

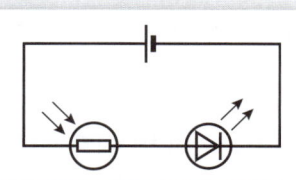

| | |
|---|---|
| In the dark the resistance of the LDR is high so the current is too low to light the LED. | |
| In the dark the resistance of the LDR is low so the current is too low to light the LED. | |
| In the light the resistance of the LDR is high so the current is high enough for the LED to light. | |

**2** Explain how a cell, thermistor and LED in series can be used to give a warning that a motor is overheating.  *(4 marks)*

# Using electrical circuits

Electrical components can be joined together in circuits to carry out useful functions.

> The examples and questions on this page use the knowledge and understanding covered by the previous pages on this topic.

## Worked example

1. (a) State what must be done to light up lamp 2 but not lamp 1 in this circuit. *(2 marks)*

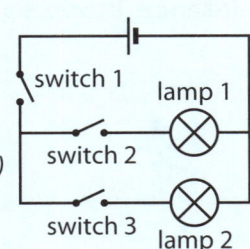

   Switches 1 and 3 must be closed and switch 2 left open.

   (b) Explain whether this type of circuit or a circuit like the one in question 1 would be best for a set of Christmas lights with many lamps. *(2 marks)*

   A parallel circuit is more useful because if some lamps are broken the others stay on.

2. Filament lamps, fluorescent lamps and LEDs are all used to provide light.

   (a) 2 C of electric charge flow though a filament lamp in 5 s and transfer 460 J of electrical energy.

   (i) Calculate the current through the lamp. *(2 marks)*

   $I$ = 2 C/5 s = 0.4 A.

   (ii) Calculate the potential difference across the lamp. *(2 marks)*

   $V$ = 460 J/2 C = 230 V

   (b) A fluorescent lamp uses a current of 0.1 A and an LED uses just 0.01 A to provide the same amount of light as the filament lamp with the same potential difference. Compare the efficiencies of the three types of light source. *(2 marks)*

   The lower the current the more efficient the light source. LEDs are much more efficient at transferring electrical energy to light than fluorescent lamps. Filament lamps have the lowest efficiency.

   > Efficiency is the percentage of the electrical energy supplied that is transferred into useful forms of energy.

   (c) LEDs are more expensive than fluorescent lamps, which are more expensive than filament lamps. Explain why LEDs and fluorescent lamps are becoming more popular. *(2 marks)*

   The better efficiency of LEDs and fluorescent lamps mean that savings in the cost of electricity outweigh the initially higher cost of the lights.

## Now try this

1. A torch has 10 LEDs, which give out the same amount of light as a torch with one filament lamp. Each LED uses 0.03 A. The LEDs are arranged in a parallel circuit.
   (a) Calculate the total current drawn from the batteries in the LED torch. *(2 marks)*
   (b) The resistance of each LED is 200 Ω. Calculate the potential difference across each LED. *(2 marks)*
   (c) State the potential difference supplied by the battery of the LED torch. *(1 mark)*

2. The torch with the filament lamp in the question above draws a current of 3 A from the same type of battery. Explain why it is more economical to use the LED torch instead of the one with the filament lamp. *(3 marks)*

   > Remember that a current is a flow of charge that takes energy from the cell.

Had a look ☐   Nearly there ☐   Nailed it! ☐

**PHYSICS 2.4.1**

# Different currents

There are some differences between the electricity from batteries and from the mains supply.

## Direct current

Cells and batteries supply DIRECT CURRENT (d.c.). This is an electric current that always travels in the same direction.

The oscilloscope trace for d.c. from a battery is a horizontal line. The potential difference can be read off the vertical scale.

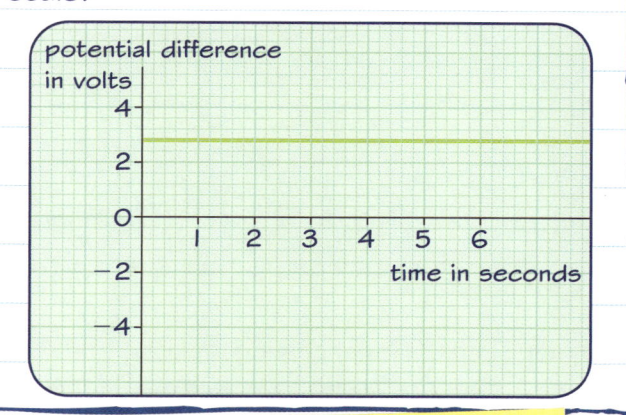

The potential difference supplied to a circuit can be shown on an oscilloscope screen.

## Alternating current

Mains electricity supplied to homes and businesses is an ALTERNATING CURRENT (a.c.). Alternating current is an electric current that changes direction regularly, and its potential difference is constantly changing.

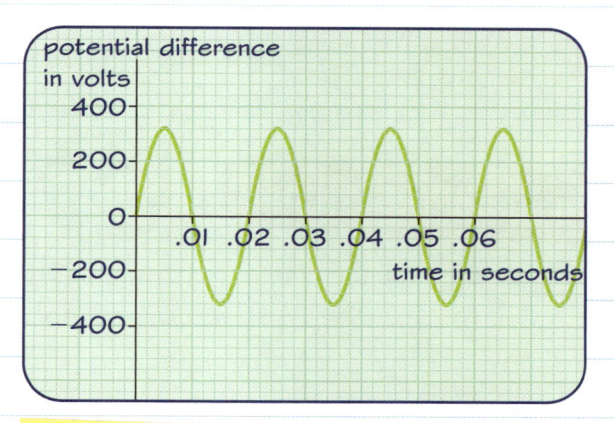

The **mean** potential difference of the mains electricity is 230 V in the UK, which is much higher than that provided by most batteries.

## Worked example (target D-C)

1. Look at the oscilloscope traces shown above.
   (a) State the potential difference of the direct current. *(1 mark)*
   
   2.4 V
   
   (b) State the highest and lowest potential difference of the alternating current. *(1 mark)*
   
   highest +320 V, lowest −320 V
   
   *This is called the peak potential difference.*
   
   (c) The frequency of the mains a.c. is 50 Hz. How many times a second does the current change direction? *(1 mark)*
   
   100
   
   *The current changes direction twice in each cycle.*

### EXAM ALERT!

Make sure that you understand the oscilloscope traces for an a.c. and d.c. supply.

Students have struggled with exam questions similar to this – **be prepared!**

## Now try this

**(target G-E)**
1. State **two** differences between the d.c. supplied by cells and the a.c. supplied by the mains. *(2 marks)*

**(target D-C)**
2. Both batteries and mains electricity have advantages. Give **one** advantage for each. *(2 marks)*

3. An a.c. source of electricity has a peak potential difference of +/−500 V. How many times in each cycle of an alternating current is the size of the potential difference 0 V? *(1 mark)*

**PHYSICS 2.4.1**  Had a look ☐   Nearly there ☐   Nailed it! ☐

# Three-pin plugs

In the UK, appliances are connected to mains electricity with a three-pin plug.

The three pins are made of a metal such as brass, which is a good electrical conductor. The inner cores of the wires are fixed to the three pins, usually by a screw.

The cable grip holds the cable firmly in the plug. This stops the wires from being pulled from the connectors.

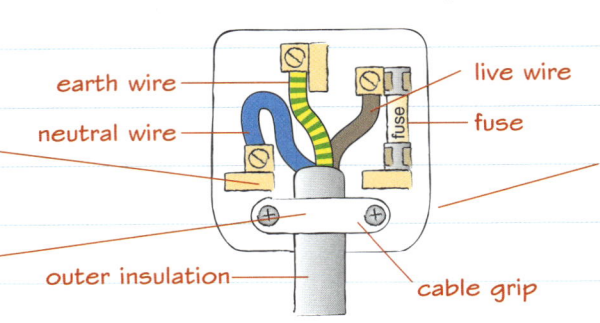

*Diagram labels:* earth wire, neutral wire, live wire, fuse, outer insulation, cable grip

See page 85 for the job done by the fuse.

The outer case of the plug is made of an insulating plastic. This stops electrical energy from being conducted to the outside of the plug.

---

## Worked example (target G–E)

**1 (a)** Describe the difference between a 2-core cable and a 3-core cable. *(2 marks)*

Two-core cables only have neutral and live wires. Three-core cables also have an earth wire.

**(b)** Explain why the inner core of a cable is made of a metal and the outer coating is plastic. *(2 marks)*

The wires are made of a metal that can conduct electrical energy. The wires are coated with plastic because it is an insulator and prevents someone getting an electric shock when they touch the cable.

**(c)** Match the colour of the plastic with the wire it is coating. *(3 marks)*

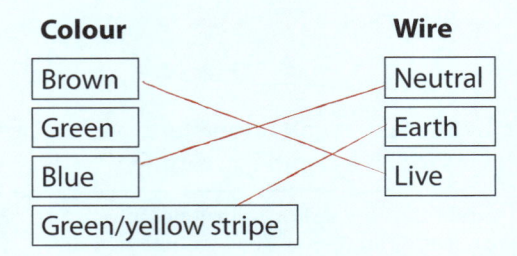

| Colour | Wire |
|---|---|
| Brown | Neutral |
| Green | Earth |
| Blue | Live |
| Green/yellow stripe | |

(Brown → Live, Blue → Neutral, Green/yellow stripe → Earth)

**2** A student fits a new three-pin plug to a music player but when she plugs it into the mains electricity it does not work. Suggest **two** reasons why the player may not be working. *(2 marks)*

The neutral or live wire may not have been fixed tightly to the pins. The earth wire may have been connected to the neutral or live pin instead of the correct wire.

There may also be a break in the neutral or live wires.

---

## Now try this

**Target G–E**

**1 (a)** State the colour of the wire connected to the following pins of a three-pin plug:
 (i) neutral   (ii) earth   *(2 marks)*
**(b)** Which pin is not connected when a two-core cable is used? *(1 mark)*

**Target D–C**

**2** Mains electricity can give a fatal electric shock if you come into contact with it. State **two** safety features of the cables and plugs used in the UK that prevent this happening. *(2 marks)*

84

Had a look ☐   Nearly there ☐   Nailed it! ☐

**PHYSICS 2.4.1**

# Electrical safety

Electrical appliances have safety features to protect users from electric shocks and fires.

## Fuses

A fuse contains a wire made of a metal with a low melting point. It is connected to the live pin in a plug. If the current is above the fuse rating of the wire the wire melts. The circuit is broken and the appliance is protected. It is important to use the right fuse in a plug. This is because if the current rating of the fuse is too low it will melt when the current flows which will be inconvenient. If the current rating of the fuse is too high then it may not protect the appliance from a larger than normal current.

## Earthing

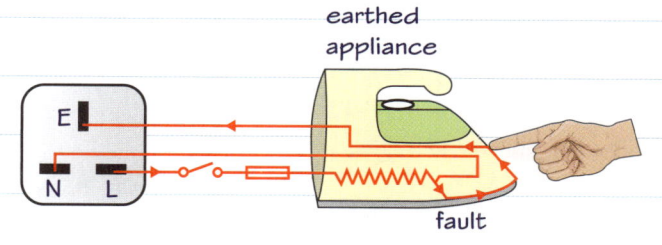

The earth wire connects the metal casing to the earth pin in the plug. If a fault connects the casing to the electric current, the earth wire conducts the current directly to the ground. The large current travelling through the earth wire causes a fuse to blow or circuit breaker to operate.

> Appliances with cases made of a non-conducting material are said to be double insulated because they have an extra layer of insulation. They do not need an earth lead.

## Worked example (target D-C)

**1 (a)** Explain how a residual current circuit breaker (RCCB) works. *(2 marks)*

The current in the neutral and live wires is normally the same. When an RCCB detects a difference between these two currents it breaks the circuit. The RCCB can be reset by pressing a switch.

**(b)** State **two** advantages of using circuit breakers instead of fuses in electrical circuits using mains electricity. *(2 marks)*

Circuit breakers cut off the current quicker than fuses. Circuit breakers can be reset, while fuses must be replaced.

> Fuses are cheaper than circuit breakers.

**2** Explain why an electric cooker needs a much thicker cable than a television. *(3 marks)*

The cooker uses a much higher current than a television. If the cooker used the same cable as the television the cable would get very hot and might cause a fire. A thicker cable can carry more current without getting as hot.

> The cooker also needs a fuse with a higher rating than the TV.

## Now try this

**1** (target G-E) Appliances require either a 3 A or 13 A fuse. State which fuse should be used in the following appliances. The figures in brackets are the current the appliance uses. *(3 marks)*

(a) kettle (12 A), (b) bedside lamp (0.25 A), (c) microwave cooker (3 A)

**2** (target D-C) Explain why it is safer to use three-core cable instead of two-core to connect an appliance with metal casing to the mains supply. *(2 marks)*

**PHYSICS 2.4.2** | Had a look ☐ | Nearly there ☐ | Nailed it! ☐

# Current and power

When an electrical charge flows through a resistor the resistor gets hot. All the components in an electrical circuit, including the wires, act as resistors.

An electrical appliance with a low efficiency wastes a lot of electrical energy raising the temperature of the components and the surroundings. Filament lamps have very low efficiency. Compact fluorescent lamps (CFLs) have a higher efficiency.

An electrical appliance has a low efficiency if most of the electrical energy is transferred to raising the temperature of the components and the surroundings. Filament lamps have a very low efficiency, while compact fluorescent lamps (CFL) waste much less electrical energy heating the surroundings.

## Power

Power is the rate at which energy is transferred.

power = energy/time

$$P = \frac{E}{t}$$

- $P$ is power in watts, W
- $E$ is energy transferred in joules, J
- $t$ is the time taken in seconds, s

The power of an electrical appliance is related to current and potential difference by the equation

power = current × potential difference

$$P = I \times V$$

- $P$ is the power in watts, W
- $I$ is the electrical current in amperes (amps), A
- $V$ is the potential difference across the appliance in volts, V

## Calculating current

The equation relating power, current and potential difference can be rearranged to give:

current = power/potential difference

$$I = \frac{P}{V}$$

The current can be calculated if the power and potential difference of an appliance are known. Once you know the current you can work out which fuse you need.

Power may be given in kilowatts, kW. 1 kW = 1000 W.

### Worked example — target D-C

**AQA SKILL Consider Page 101**

1. A family wants to buy a new refrigerator. Two models of the same size are available. Discuss **one** factor the family need to think about to help them choose which model to buy. *(2 marks)*

They should check the efficiency of the models. The one with the highest efficiency will waste the least amount of electrical energy. It will use less electrical power and cost less to run.

### Now try this

**target D-C**

1. A filament lamp and compact fluorescent lamp (CFL) both use mains electricity (potential difference = 230 V) and give out the same amount of light energy. The filament lamp has a power of 100 W. The current through the CFL is 0.1 A.
   (a) Calculate the power of the CFL. *(2 marks)*
   (b) Explain why the CFL is more efficient than the filament lamp. *(2 marks)*

**target D-C**

2. A kettle using mains electricity (230V) uses a current of 8.7 A.
   (a) Calculate the power of the kettle. *(2 marks)*
   (b) 3A and 13A fuses are available. Explain which one should be used in the plug for the kettle. *(2 marks)*

Had a look ☐   Nearly there ☐   Nailed it! ☐   **PHYSICS**

# Physics six mark question 2

There will be one 6 mark question on your exam paper, which will be marked for *quality of written communication* as well as scientific knowledge. This means that you need to apply your scientific knowledge, present your answer in a logical and organised way, and make sure that your spelling, grammar and punctuation are as good as you can make them.

## Worked example

An electric shock from mains electricity at 230 V can kill. Explain the safety precautions that ensure people can use mains electric appliances without receiving shocks.

(6 marks)

An appliance is connected to the mains electricity supply by a cable and three-pin plug. The cable has two layers of insulation, with an outer coating of plastic around the two or three wires. Each wire also has a coating of plastic, preventing any short circuits.

The three-pin plug has an outer casing of insulating plastic. The cable is held firmly by a cable grip to stop the wires from being pulled from their connectors.

Many appliances are double insulated, with their casings made of an insulator. Appliances with a metal casing must use a three-core cable with a wire connected to the earth pin of the plug. This connects the earth wire to the ground. If a fault connects the metal casing to the circuit, the earth wire carries the current to the ground instead of it passing through a person touching the casing.

Plugs have a fuse that melts and breaks the circuit if a fault causes the current to rise. The rating of the fuse must be chosen to be just above the normal current.

The mains circuit will also be fitted with a fuse or a circuit breaker (RCCB). The circuit breaker detects abnormally large currents and breaks the circuit before any harm can be done.

### Recall and explain

You need to recall the various safety measures that are taken and explain how they prevent electric shocks.

Remember that an electric current will pass more easily through a conductor, such as a metal, than an insulator, such as a plastic.

Plan your answer before writing it down. Here there are a number of safety precautions to consider such as the cable, three-pin plugs, double insulation, earthing, fuses and circuit breakers.

The answer explains how each safety precaution prevents the user from coming into contact with the electric current.

You should describe the properties of filament lamps and LEDs and explain why LEDs are becoming more popular.

## Now try this

Filament lamps provided our lighting for well over 100 years. Today LEDs are slowly replacing filament lamps in homes, shops and offices. Evaluate the use of filament lamps and LEDs.

(6 marks)

— ⊗ — lamp

— ⊕ — LED

**PHYSICS 2.5.1** — Had a look ☐ Nearly there ☐ Nailed it! ☐

# Atomic structure

## The nuclear atom

Atoms have a tiny central NUCLEUS, which has a positive charge. The nucleus is made up of PROTONS and NEUTRONS. The nucleus is surrounded by ELECTRONS.

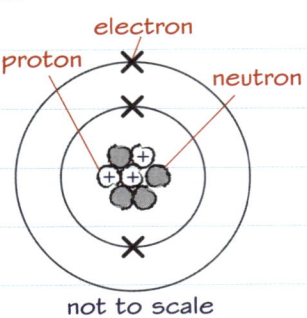

| Particle | Charge | Relative mass | Position in atom |
|---|---|---|---|
| proton | +1 | 1 | nucleus |
| neutron | 0 | 1 | nucleus |
| electron | −1 | very small | in orbits around nucleus |

An atom is mostly empty space. If an atom was the size of an Olympic stadium, the nucleus would be the size of a football.

## Atoms and ions

The number of protons is the same as the number of electrons, so an atom does not have an overall electric charge.

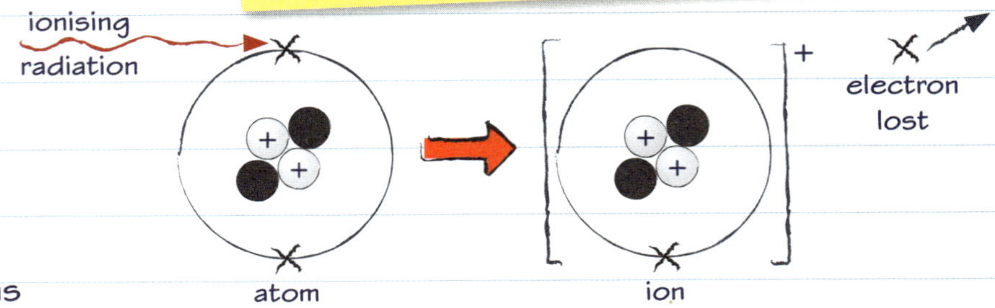

Atoms can lose or gain electrons to form charged particles called ions. When electrons are gained the ion has a negative charge. When electrons are lost the ion has a positive charge.

## Worked example (target D-C)

(a) What is the atomic number of deuterium?   **1**   (1 mark)

Atomic number is the number of protons in the atom.

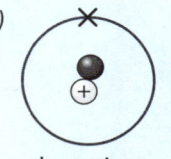

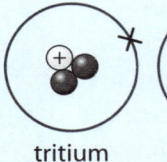

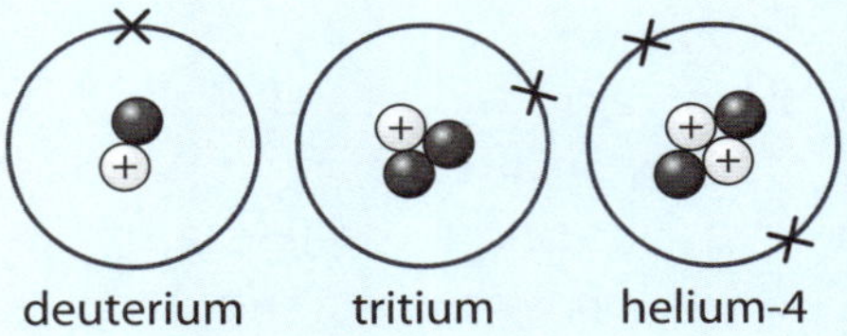

(b) What is the mass number of helium?   **4**   (1 mark)

Mass number is the total number of protons and neutrons in the atom. The mass of electrons is so small that they are ignored in the mass number.

(c) State why deuterium and tritium are isotopes.   (2 marks)

They have the same number of protons but a different number of neutrons.

## Now try this

**1** (target G-E) Name the particles in an atom that:
  (a) have the same mass   (1 mark)
  (b) are charged   (1 mark)
  (c) orbit the nucleus   (1 mark)

**2** (target D-C) Atoms of element X have an atomic number of 3 and mass number of 7.
  (a) How many protons, neutrons and electrons do the atoms have?   (3 marks)
  (b) Particle Y is an ion of element X with a charge of +1. Describe how the structure of particle Y is similar to and different from atoms of element X.   (2 marks)

Had a look ☐   Nearly there ☐   Nailed it! ☐    **PHYSICS 2.5.2**

# Background radiation

We are constantly receiving radiation from our surroundings. Some substances give out RADIATION from their unstable nuclei. These substances are said to be RADIOACTIVE. The process is not affected by temperature or by chemical reactions.

RADIOACTIVE DECAY is a random process. This means it is impossible to predict when a particular nucleus will give out radiation.

Most cosmic rays are stopped by the atmosphere.

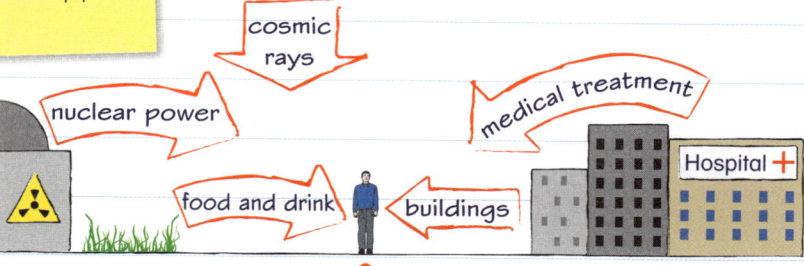

cosmic rays • nuclear power • medical treatment • food and drink • buildings • radon gas from earth

Radon gas is released into the air by certain types of rock.

Most of the sources of background radiation are natural, but a few are man-made, such as radiation from medical procedures and nuclear power (including nuclear accidents and tests of nuclear weapons).

## Worked example  (target D–C)

The data in the table compare the dose of radiation received by people in a year with the average annual dose in the UK.

|  | Annual radiation dose |
|---|---|
| UK average | 1 |
| Residents of Cornwall | 3 |
| Coal miners | 2 |

Some of the rocks in Cornwall release radon gas.

**(a)** Comment on the effect of where you live on your radiation dose. *(2 marks)*

Radiation dose varies from place to place and is higher in Cornwall than the average for the UK.

**(b)** Discuss the effect of where you work on your radiation dose. *(2 marks)*

Some jobs result in a higher-than-average dose of radiation. Coal miners receive a higher dose because they are surrounded by rocks that give out radiation.

## Now try this

**target G–E**

**1 (a)** Name **one** natural source of background radiation. *(1 mark)*
 **(b)** Name **one** man-made source of background radiation. *(1 mark)*

**target D–C**

**2 (a)** State why it is not possible to say exactly when an unstable atom will decay. *(1 mark)*
 **(b)** It is recommended that people who live or work in basements in some areas of the UK should fit fans in the walls. Suggest why this recommendation is made. *(2 marks)*

# Alpha, beta and gamma radiation

## Types of radiation

An unstable nucleus can give out different types of radiation.

(α) alpha particles
- will travel a few centimetres in air
- very ionising
- can be stopped by a sheet of paper

(β) beta particles
- will travel a few metres in air
- moderately ionising
- can be stopped by 3 mm thick aluminium

(γ) gamma rays
- will travel a few kilometres in air
- weakly ionising
- need thick lead to stop them

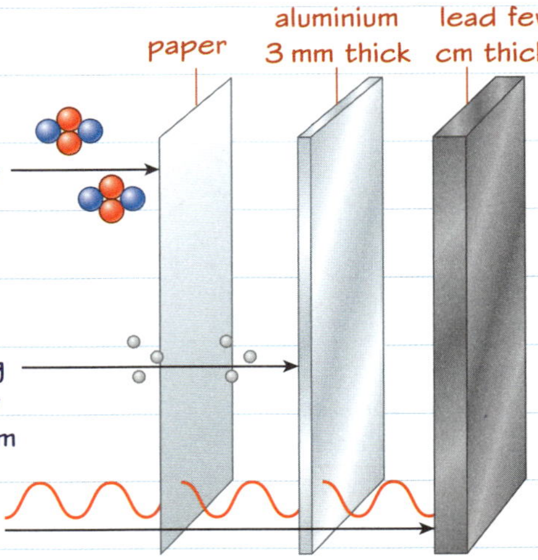

Alpha radiation is particles made up of two protons and two neutrons, like the nucleus of a helium atom.

Beta radiation is electrons given off from the nucleus.

Gamma radiation is electromagnetic radiation with a very short wavelength.

Alpha, beta and gamma are ionising radiation. This means they have the ability to add or remove electrons from atoms that they hit, which turns the atoms into ions.

### EXAM ALERT!

You need to learn the properties of the three types of radiation.

Students have struggled with exam questions similar to this – **be prepared!**

## Worked example

The diagram shows what happens when alpha, beta and gamma radiation pass through an electric field.

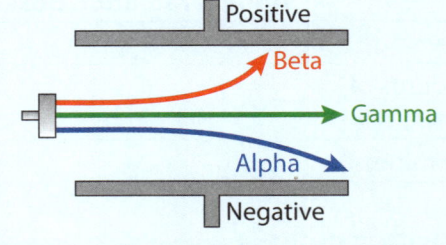

(a) Which type of radiation is not deflected by an electric field? *(1 mark)*

gamma

(b) Which type of radiation is deflected the most by an electric field? *(1 mark)*

beta

(c) Alpha and beta radiation are deflected in the same direction by an electric field. Is this statement true or false? *(1 mark)*

false

Each of the three types of radiation behave in the same way in magnetic fields as they do in electric fields.

## Now try this

1. Name the type of radiation that:
   (a) is a helium nucleus;  (b) travels the furthest through the atmosphere;
   (c) is negatively charged. *(3 marks)*

2. Give **three** differences between the properties of alpha and beta radiation. *(3 marks)*

Had a look ☐    Nearly there ☐    Nailed it! ☐    **PHYSICS 2.5.2**

# Half-life

The activity of a radioactive material decreases with time.

The HALF-LIFE of a radioactive isotope is the average time taken for the number of nuclei of the isotope in the sample to halve.

Alternatively, if we measure the count rate of a sample containing a radioactive isotope, the half-life is the time taken for the count rate to fall to half its initial level.

> Count rate is the number of nuclear decays that happen every second.

> Tracers can be used to trace the flow of a substance. You will find out more about the uses of radiation on page 92.

### Plotting half-lives

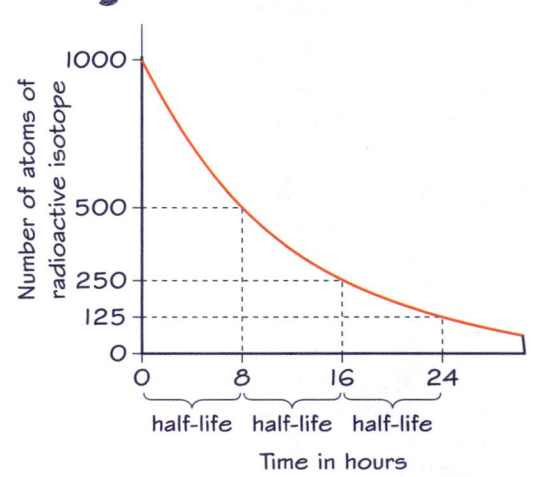

[Graph: Number of atoms of radioactive isotope vs Time in hours. Values 1000, 500, 250, 125, 0 on y-axis; 0, 8, 16, 24 on x-axis. Each 8-hour interval marked as a half-life.]

The graph shows how the count rate of a sample changes with time. It has a half-life of 8 hours. At the end of each 8-hour period the count rate falls to half what it was at the start of that period.

---

| Radioactive isotopes are used as TRACERS. In hospital, they are injected into a patient and carried to cancer cells. | → | The radiation can be detected by a gamma camera and shows where the cancer cells are in the patient's body. | → | The half-life of the radioactive isotope must be long enough so that there is time for it to reach the cancer cells before it decays. The half-life must be short enough so that soon there is very little radioactive material left in the body. A half-life of a few hours is suitable. |

---

## Worked example    target D-C

**AQA SKILL Evaluate Page 101**

A water company puts a radioactive isotope into an underground water pipe. They want to detect radiation at the point where water is leaking from the pipe. Give a reason why a half-life of the isotope of 2 hours is suitable for this purpose. *(2 marks)*

*The half-life is long enough for there still to be enough activity to measure when the isotope reaches the leak, but it is short enough so that the water does not remain radioactive for long enough to harm people.*

---

## Now try this

**target G-E**
**target D-C**

1. Look at the graph at the top of the page. Explain why the count rate falls from 1000 to 250 in 16 hours. *(2 marks)*
2. A radioactive isotope of technetium (Tc) is used in hospitals to detect cancers. When injected into the patient the isotope has a count rate of 80 counts/minute. After 12 hours the isotope is producing 20 counts/minute.
   (a) Calculate the half-life of the radioactive isotope. *(2 marks)*
   (b) Explain why this half-life is suitable for its purpose. *(2 marks)*

**PHYSICS 2.5.2**  Had a look ☐  Nearly there ☐  Nailed it! ☐

# Uses and dangers

There are many uses for each type of nuclear radiation, but there are hazards too.

## Risks from radiation

Alpha is the least penetrating and cannot pass through skin, but as it is the most ionising it could cause most damage to cells if the source is inside the body. Gamma is the least ionising so causes the least damage but is the most penetrating so is harmful when the source is outside the body. Beta falls between alpha and gamma in penetration and ionising strength.

## Uses of alpha, beta and gamma radiation

A source of alpha radiation is used in smoke alarms.

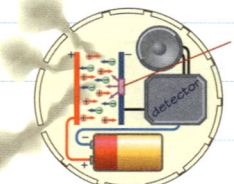

Source of radiation gives off a constant stream of alpha particles.

Alpha radiation produces ions in the air that complete the electric circuit. Smoke particles absorb the alpha particles so the circuit is broken, and this sets off the alarm.

**USES OF RADIATION**

In cancer treatment powerful beams of gamma rays are sent from various directions to focus on the cancerous cells, so these cells receive more radiation than the surrounding, healthy cells.

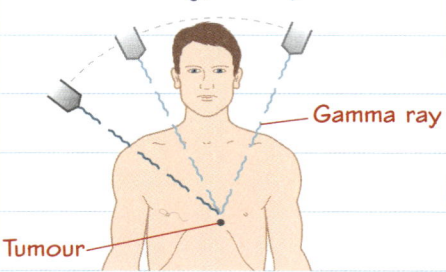

— Gamma ray
— Tumour

Beta radiation is used to monitor the thickness of paper and to control the filling of cartons. When paper is too thick not as many beta particles pass through the paper to reach the detector. A processor increases the force on rollers to make the paper thinner. If the paper is too thin, more beta particles get through.

Gamma radiation is used for the treatment and detection of cancers because it can travel through the body and causes the least harm to healthy cells.

### Worked example (target G-E)

**1** Give **four** precautions to take in order to reduce the exposure to radiation from radioactive materials. *(4 marks)*

Radioactive materials should be stored in a lead lined box. Long handled tongs should be used to move samples. Protective clothing should be worn. Breathing apparatus should be used to stop inhaling radioactive material.

### Now try this

**1** Match the type of radiation to the use. *(3 marks)* (target G-E)

- alpha
- beta
- gamma

- finding a leak in a buried gas pipe
- checking that cardboard cartons of breakfast cereal are filled
- night-vision goggles
- smoke alarms fitted in houses

**2** Explain why a source of gamma radiation is the most suitable for injection into a patient to find where a cancer tumour is located. *(2 marks)* (target D-C)

Had a look ☐   Nearly there ☐   Nailed it! ☐

**PHYSICS 2.5.1**

# The nuclear model of the atom

Radiation from a radioactive isotope was used to investigate the structure of the atom.

## Ideas about atoms

Until the 1890s people thought of atoms as hard balls. The discovery of the electron suggested that atoms had structure. The first theory was that atoms were like plum puddings or currant buns.

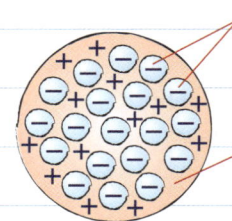

- Tiny, negatively charged electrons were the plums or currants.
- The 'pudding' took up the space of the atom and had the positive charge and almost all of its mass.

## Rutherford and Marsden

In 1909 Rutherford and Marsden repeated an experiment in which alpha particles were passed through a sheet of gold leaf. Unlike other scientists they checked to see if any alpha particles were deflected by large angles. They did not expect to find anything new, but they did find that a few alpha particle bounced almost straight back from the gold atoms.

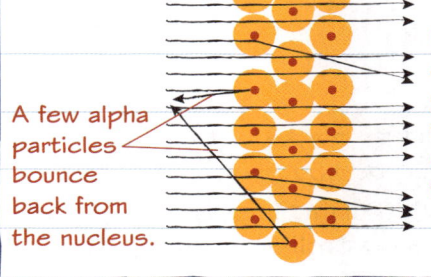

- A few alpha particles bounce back from the nucleus.
- Most of the alpha radiation passes through the atom without touching the nucleus.

## Rutherford's new idea

Rutherford realised that the plum pudding model could not explain the new evidence. He suggested instead that most of the atom was empty space. Right at the centre of the atom was a very small but very dense positively charged nucleus. This is called the nuclear model of the atom. (See page 88.)

### Worked example

**target G-E**

1 Complete the sentences below by circling the correct answer.

(a) In the plum pudding model of the atom the mass is mainly

   at the edge of    at the centre of
   (**all through**)

   the atom.   *(1 mark)*

(b) The Rutherford–Marsden experiment showed that the positive charge in the atom was   *(1 mark)*

   (**in the nucleus**)   spread out    around the outside

### Now try this

**target G-E**

1 Which **one** of the following results surprised Rutherford and Marsden in the alpha scattering experiment?
   *(1 mark)*

   A: Most of the alpha radiation went straight through the gold leaf.

   B: Some alpha radiation bounced back.

   C: The gold leaf did not absorb the alpha particles.

**target D-C**

2 Explain why the nuclear model of the atom replaced the plum pudding model of the atom.   *(2 marks)*

**PHYSICS 2.6.1** | Had a look ☐ | Nearly there ☐ | Nailed it! ☐

# Nuclear fission

Nuclear fission releases energy that is used in nuclear power stations.

In nuclear fission the nucleus of an atom splits into two smaller nuclei and energy is transferred.

A few nuclei are fissionable, including uranium-235 and plutonium-239. The uranium isotope is the one normally used in nuclear reactors for generating electricity.

The numbers are the mass numbers of the isotopes.

If the neutrons are absorbed by other fissionable nuclei the reaction can happen again. This is the start of a chain reaction where the neutrons produced go on to cause other nuclear fission reactions.

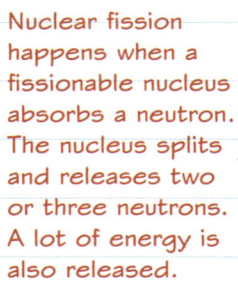

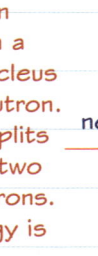

Energy is released as radiation and in heating the surroundings.

Nuclear fission happens when a fissionable nucleus absorbs a neutron. The nucleus splits and releases two or three neutrons. A lot of energy is also released.

neutron → uranium-235 → energy release → daughter nuclei / three neutrons released

In a nuclear power station, two of the neutrons are absorbed by other materials, so that only one neutron from each fission can cause a new reaction. This is a **controlled chain reaction**.

## Worked example (target D-C)

Use the information in the diagram to describe how nuclear fission is used to generate electrical energy in a nuclear power station.

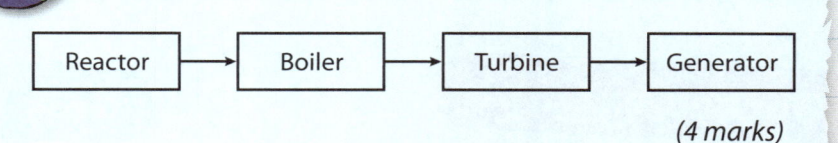

Reactor → Boiler → Turbine → Generator

(4 marks)

Fission takes place in the nuclear reactor and releases heat energy. In the boiler the heat energy turns water into steam. In the turbine the heat energy of the steam makes the turbines turn, giving them kinetic energy. In the generator the kinetic energy is transferred to electrical energy.

## Now try this (target D-C)

1. Which **one** of the following nuclei can undergo a fission reaction in a nuclear reactor? (1 mark)
   A: hydrogen-2   B: uranium-235   C: uranium-238   D: radium-226

2. In a nuclear power station the fission of uranium-235 nuclei takes place in a controlled chain reaction. Explain, using a sketch diagram, how this occurs. (3 marks)

Had a look ☐  Nearly there ☐  Nailed it! ☐   **PHYSICS 2.6.2**

# Nuclear fusion

Nuclear fusion is the process that makes stars shine.

Nuclear fusion is the joining together of two atomic nuclei to form a single larger atomic nucleus.

Nuclear fusion reactions release a lot of energy.

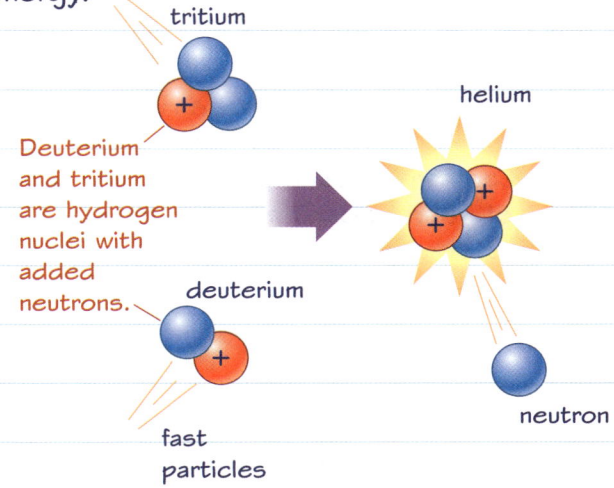

Deuterium and tritium are hydrogen nuclei with added neutrons.

Two hydrogen nuclei can join together to form a helium nucleus.

## Fusion in stars

Fusion produces atoms of heavier elements.

Hydrogen nuclei were formed shortly after the Universe formed in the Big Bang. In stable stars nuclear fusion reactions form all the elements up to iron.

Some stars explode in a supernova at the end of their life. This is when nuclear fusion reactions form the elements heavier than iron.

### EXAM ALERT!

Don't confuse nuclear fission and nuclear fusion. 'Fission' means splitting and 'fusion' means joining together.

Students have struggled with exam questions similar to this – **be prepared!**

Nuclear fusion only takes place at extremely high temperatures and pressures such as are found in stars.

### Worked example  *target D-C*

1  Compare the uses that are made of nuclear fission and nuclear fusion.
(2 marks)

Nuclear fission is widely used to generate electricity in nuclear power stations. Nuclear fusion is not used at present for peaceful purposes.

### Now try this

1  *target G-E* Which **one** of the following is the heaviest element formed in stable stars?
(1 mark)
A: hydrogen
B: carbon
C: uranium
D: iron

2  *target D-C*
(a) Explain why the Universe today contains many different elements, even though the Big Bang is thought to have produced only hydrogen nuclei. (2 marks)
(b) Explain how nuclei as heavy as gold and uranium are formed. (2 marks)

**PHYSICS 2.6.2**    Had a look ☐    Nearly there ☐    Nailed it! ☐

# The lifecycle of stars

The lifecycle of stars lasts millions or billions of years.

## The birth of stars

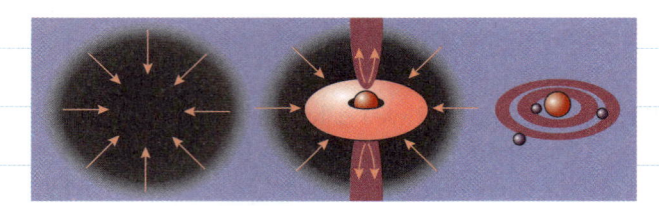

Gases and dust in space are attracted together by the force of GRAVITY.

If the ball of matter is big enough, FUSION reactions start and a PROTOSTAR is formed. This becomes a MAIN SEQUENCE star.

Small masses may also form and be attracted by a larger mass to form PLANETS.

The size of the star decides what will happen to it during its lifecycle, as shown below.

Stars like the Sun remain stable for billions of years. The gravitational forces pulling the matter in are balanced by other forces that try to make the star expand.

Fusion reactions turn hydrogen into other, heavier elements, step by step. These fusion reactions keep the star shining for billions of years. Stars are so massive they have enough matter to last for their lifetime.

---

The dust and gases that form a **protostar** come from the matter thrown out by earlier stars.

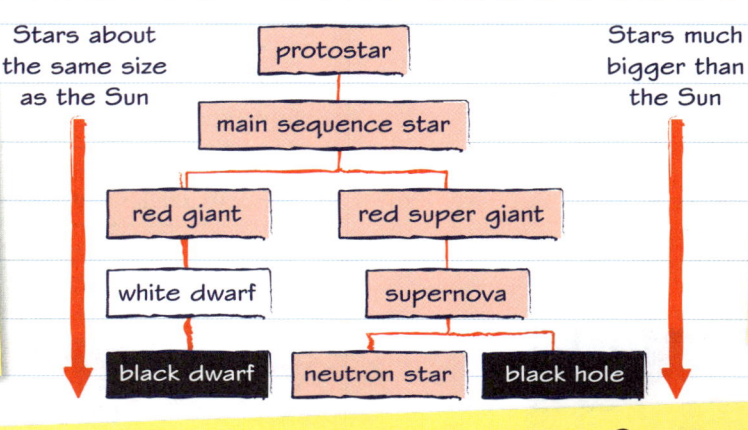

Stars about the same size as the Sun → protostar → main sequence star → red giant → white dwarf → black dwarf

Stars much bigger than the Sun → protostar → main sequence star → red super giant → supernova → neutron star / black hole

A **supernova** is a huge explosion where a star throws out most of its mass.

Don't confuse **black dwarf** stars with **black holes**. Our sun will eventually become a black dwarf when the fusion reactions in it stop. Only extremely large stars eventually form black holes.

---

## Worked example (target D-C)

Compare how neutron stars, black dwarves and black holes are formed. *(2 marks)*

Black dwarves are formed by smaller stars at the end of their life. Neutron stars and black holes are formed after the supernova of much larger stars.

---

## Now try this

**1** (target G-E) Put the following stages of a star's lifecycle into the correct order. *(3 marks)*

| white dwarf    main sequence star    black dwarf    protostar    red giant |

**2** (target D-C) The Sun has been shining for over 5 billion years and is only halfway through its lifecycle. Explain why stars like the Sun can shine for so long. *(2 marks)*

Had a look ☐   Nearly there ☐   Nailed it! ☐   **PHYSICS**

# Physics six mark question 3

There will be one 6 mark question on your exam paper, which will be marked for *quality of written communication* as well as scientific knowledge. This means that you need to apply your scientific knowledge, present your answer in a logical and organised way, and make sure that your spelling, grammar and punctuation are as good as you can make them.

---

### Worked example

Nuclear fission and nuclear fusion are processes that involve the nuclei of atoms. Compare the two processes.

*(6 marks)*

Nuclear fission involves the splitting of a heavy nucleus of, for example, uranium-235 or plutonium-239. The reaction starts when the nucleus absorbs a neutron. The nucleus splits into two smaller nuclei and gives out two or three neutrons. These neutrons can go on to set off more fission reactions. This starts a chain reaction.

Nuclear fusion takes place when nuclei join together to form larger nuclei – for example, when hydrogen nuclei join to form helium nuclei.

Both processes release a large amount of energy as heat and sometimes as radiation.

The nuclei of only a few isotopes can take part in fission reactions, while all the isotopes of elements heavier than hydrogen are produced by and take part in fusion reactions in the stars.

Nuclear fission reactions can be controlled and have been used in nuclear power stations for decades. Nuclear fusion takes place in stars but has not yet been put into use to produce power on Earth.

### Compare

To answer a question that asks you to COMPARE nuclear fission and nuclear fusion you must first describe the two processes and then point out the similarities and the differences between them.

> This is a good answer because it contains both similarities and differences.

> This is the hazard symbol for radiation.

> Think about the harm radiation can cause, the properties of the different types of radiation and why various safety precautions are effective.

---

### Now try this

We are exposed to nuclear radiation from the natural background and from the uses made of radioactive materials. Compare the hazards from different types of radiation and the precautions taken to limit exposure.

*(6 marks)*

# Periodic Table

**Key**
relative atomic mass
**atomic symbol**
name
atomic (proton) number

Example: 1 **H** hydrogen 1

| 1 | 2 | | | | | | | | | | | 3 | 4 | 5 | 6 | 7 | 0 |
|---|---|---|---|---|---|---|---|---|---|---|---|---|---|---|---|---|---|
| | | | | | | | | | | | | | | | | | 4 **He** helium 2 |
| 7 **Li** lithium 3 | 9 **Be** beryllium 4 | | | | | | | | | | | 11 **B** boron 5 | 12 **C** carbon 6 | 14 **N** nitrogen 7 | 16 **O** oxygen 8 | 19 **F** fluorine 9 | 20 **Ne** neon 10 |
| 23 **Na** sodium 11 | 24 **Mg** magnesium 12 | | | | | | | | | | | 27 **Al** aluminium 13 | 28 **Si** silicon 14 | 31 **P** phosphorous 15 | 32 **S** sulfur 16 | 35.5 **Cl** chlorine 17 | 40 **Ar** argon 18 |
| 39 **K** potassium 19 | 40 **Ca** calcium 20 | 45 **Sc** scandium 21 | 48 **Ti** titanium 22 | 51 **V** vanadium 23 | 52 **Cr** chromium 24 | 55 **Mn** manganese 25 | 56 **Fe** iron 26 | 59 **Co** cobalt 27 | 59 **Ni** nickel 28 | 63.5 **Cu** copper 29 | 65 **Zn** zinc 30 | 70 **Ga** gallium 31 | 73 **Ge** germanium 32 | 75 **As** arsenic 33 | 79 **Se** selenium 34 | 80 **Br** bromine 35 | 84 **Kr** krypton 36 |
| 85 **Rb** rubidium 37 | 88 **Sr** strontium 38 | 89 **Y** yttrium 39 | 91 **Zr** zirconium 40 | 93 **Nb** niobium 41 | 96 **Mo** molybdenum 42 | 99 **Tc** technetium 43 | 101 **Ru** ruthenium 44 | 103 **Rh** rhodium 45 | 106 **Pd** palladium 46 | 108 **Ag** silver 47 | 112 **Cd** cadmium 48 | 115 **In** indium 49 | 119 **Sn** tin 50 | 122 **Sb** antimony 51 | 128 **Te** tellurium 52 | 127 **I** iodine 53 | 131 **Xe** xenon 54 |
| 133 **Cs** caesium 55 | 137 **Ba** barium 56 | 139 **La** lanthanum 57 | 178 **Hf** hafnium 72 | 181 **Ta** tantalum 73 | 184 **W** tungsten 74 | 186 **Re** rhenium 75 | 190 **Os** osmium 76 | 192 **Ir** iridium 77 | 195 **Pt** platinum 78 | 197 **Au** gold 79 | 201 **Hg** mercury 80 | 204 **Tl** thallium 81 | 207 **Pb** lead 82 | 209 **Bi** bismuth 83 | 210 **Po** polonium 84 | 211 **At** astatine 85 | 222 **Rn** radon 86 |
| 223 **Fr** francium 87 | 226 **Ra** radium 88 | 227 **Ac** actinium 89 | 261 **Rf** rutherfordium 104 | 262 **Db** dubnium 105 | 266 **Sg** seaborgium 106 | 264 **Bh** bohrium 107 | 277 **Hs** hassium 108 | 268 **Mt** meitnerium 109 | 271 **Ds** darmstadtium 110 | 272 **Rg** roentgenium 111 | | | | | | | |

The lanthanides (atomic numbers 58–71) and the actinides (atomic numbers 58–71) have been omitted.
Elements with atomic numbers 112–118 have been reported but not fully authenticated.
Cu and Cl have not been rounded to the nearest number.

# Chemistry Data Sheet

## Reactivity series of metals

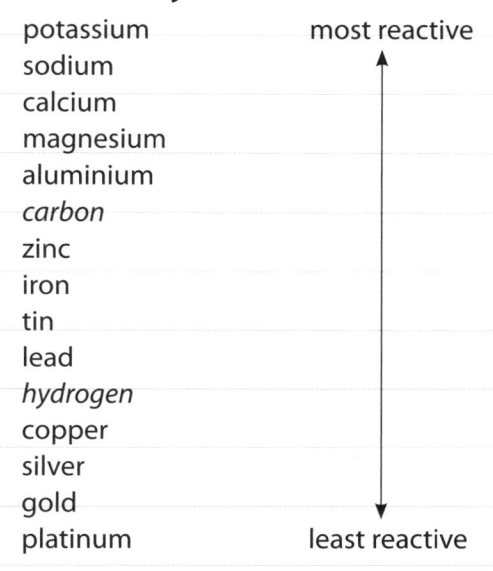

potassium — most reactive
sodium
calcium
magnesium
aluminium
*carbon*
zinc
iron
tin
lead
*hydrogen*
copper
silver
gold
platinum — least reactive

Elements in italics, though non-metals, have been included for comparison.

## Formulae of some common ions

**Positive ions**

| Name | Formula |
|---|---|
| hydrogen | $H^+$ |
| sodium | $Na^+$ |
| silver | $Ag^+$ |
| potassium | $K^+$ |
| lithium | $Li^+$ |
| ammonium | $NH_4^+$ |
| barium | $Ba^{2+}$ |
| calcium | $Ca^{2+}$ |
| copper(II) | $Cu^{2+}$ |
| magnesium | $Mg^{2+}$ |
| zinc | $Zn^{2+}$ |
| lead | $Pb^{2+}$ |
| iron(II) | $Fe^{2+}$ |
| iron(III) | $Fe^{3+}$ |
| aluminium | $Al^{3+}$ |

**Negative ions**

| Name | Formula |
|---|---|
| chloride | $Cl^-$ |
| bromide | $Br^-$ |
| fluoride | $F^-$ |
| iodide | $I^-$ |
| hydroxide | $OH^-$ |
| nitrate | $NO_3^-$ |
| oxide | $O^{2-}$ |
| sulfide | $S^{2-}$ |
| sulfate | $SO_4^{2-}$ |
| carbonate | $CO_3^{2-}$ |

# Physics Equation Sheet

| Equation | Symbols |
|---|---|
| $a = \dfrac{F}{m}$ or $F = m \times a$ | $F$ resultant force<br>$m$ mass<br>$a$ acceleration |
| $a = \dfrac{v - u}{t}$ | $a$ acceleration<br>$v$ final velocity<br>$u$ initial velocity<br>$t$ time taken |
| $W = m \times g$ | $W$ weight<br>$m$ mass<br>$g$ gravitational field strength |
| $F = k \times e$ | $F$ force<br>$k$ spring constant<br>$e$ extension |
| $W = F \times d$ | $W$ work done<br>$F$ force applied<br>$d$ distance moved in the direction of the force |
| $P = \dfrac{E}{t}$ | $P$ power<br>$E$ energy transferred<br>$t$ time taken |
| $E_p = m \times g \times h$ | $E_p$ change in gravitational potential energy<br>$m$ mass<br>$g$ gravitational field strength<br>$h$ change in height |
| $E_k = \dfrac{1}{2} \times m \times v^2$ | $E_k$ kinetic energy<br>$m$ mass<br>$v$ speed |
| $p = m \times v$ | $p$ momentum<br>$m$ mass<br>$v$ velocity |
| $I = \dfrac{Q}{t}$ | $I$ current<br>$Q$ charge<br>$t$ time |
| $V = \dfrac{W}{Q}$ | $V$ potential difference<br>$W$ work done<br>$Q$ charge |
| $V = I \times R$ | $V$ potential difference<br>$I$ current<br>$R$ resistance |
| $P = I \times V$ | $P$ power<br>$I$ current<br>$V$ potential difference |
| $E = V \times Q$ | $E$ energy<br>$V$ potential difference (Higher Tier only)<br>$Q$ charge |

# AQA specification skills

In your AQA exam there are certain **skills** that you sometimes need to **apply** when answering a question. Questions often contain a particular **command word** that lets you know this. On this page we explain how to spot a command word and how to apply the required skill.

> Note: Watch out for our Spec Skills sticker — this points out the Worked Examples that are particularly focussed on applying skills.

| Command word | Skill you are being asked to apply |
| --- | --- |
| **Apply** | You might be asked to **apply** what you know about a topic to a practical situation. For example: 'Apply your knowledge of series and parallel circuits to suggest the best wiring for a set of Christmas tree lights.' |
| **Compare** | **Compare** how two things are similar or different. Make sure you include both of the things you are being asked to compare. For example: 'A is bigger than B, but B is lighter than A.' |
| **Consider** | You will be given some information and you will be asked to **consider** all the factors that might influence a decision. For example: 'When buying a new fridge the family would need to consider the following things …' |
| **Describe** | **Describe** a process or why something happens in an accurate way. For example: 'When coal is burned the heat energy is used to turn water into steam. The steam is then used to turn a turbine …' |
| **Discuss** | In some questions you might be asked to make an informed judgement about a topic. This might be something like stem cell research. You should **discuss** the topic and give your **opinion** but make sure that you back it up with information from the question or your scientific knowledge. |
| **Draw** | Some questions ask you to **draw** or sketch something. It might be the electrons in an atom, a graph or a ray diagram. Make sure you take a pencil, rubber and ruler into your exam. |
| **Evaluate** | This is the most important one! Most of the skill statements start with **evaluate**. You will be given information and will be expected to use that information plus anything you know from studying the material in the specification to look at evidence and come to a **conclusion**. For example, if you were asked to evaluate which of two slimming programmes was better, then you might comment like this: 'In programme A people lost weight quickly to start with but then put the weight back on by the end of the sixth month. In programme B they did not lose weight so quickly to start with, but the weight loss was slow and steady and no weight was gained back by the end of the year. I therefore think that programme B is most effective.' |
| **Explain** | State what is happening and **explain** why it is happening. If a question asks you to explain then it is a good idea to try to use the word 'because' in your answer. For example: 'pH 2 is the optimal pH for enzymes in the stomach because the stomach is very acidic.' |
| **Formulae** | In some chemistry questions you will be expected to write chemical **formulae** for compounds. You will be given the symbols and the ions can be found on the Data Sheet on page 99. |

# SKILLS STICKERS

| Command word | Skill you are being asked to apply |
|---|---|
| **Interpret** (AQA SKILL, Page 101) | **Interpret** the data given to you on graphs, diagrams or in tables to help answer the question. For example: 'Use the data to show what happens when …' |
| **Predict** (AQA SKILL, Page 101) | A question may ask you to **predict** the outcome of a genetic cross or what will be formed at different electrodes in an electrolysis experiment. If you learn the patterns of genetic crosses and the rules about electrolysis then you will be able to do this. |
| **Suggest** (AQA SKILL, Page 101) | You will be given some information about an unfamiliar situation and asked to **suggest** an answer to a question. You will not have learned the answer – you need to **apply** your knowledge to that new situation. For example: 'I think that blue is better than green because …' or 'It might be because …' |

Had a look ☐   Nearly there ☐   Nailed it! ☐

**ISA SUPPORT**

# ISA support

25% of each Science GCSE comes from controlled assessments called ISAs (Investigative Skills Assignments). These have four stages:

1. Carrying out some research to plan an experiment to investigate a hypothesis.
2. ISA Paper 1: a 45-minute question paper about your experiment plan done under exam conditions.
3. Carrying out your experiment (or a similar one with instructions provided by your teacher).
4. ISA Paper 2: a 50-minute question paper about your results and some similar case studies done under exam conditions.

All the examples on this page are from an investigation into measuring how changing the load on a spring affects the stretch (extension) of the spring.

## Worked example

**Hypothesis (Paper 1)**

1. Write a hypothesis about how mass affects the length of a spring. Use information from your scientific knowledge or research to explain why you made this hypothesis.

Hypothesis – I predict that the spring will stretch more as more masses are added.

Explanation – This is because the mass exerts a pulling force downwards on the spring called weight. The greater the mass, the greater the weight and so the greater the force pulling down on the spring.

> The hypothesis is very sensible and is justified with some good science. The student has clearly explained why increasing the load will increase the stretch, not just why changing the load will change the stretch.

**Research sources (Paper 1)**

2. Name two sources you used for your research. Which sources did you find most useful and why?

My sources were:
1. AQA GCSE Physics (editor Nigel English)
2. http://www.nuffieldfoundation.org/practical-physics/investigating-simple-steel-springs

Source 1 was useful because it explained the science theory of how the load affects how far the spring stretches. Source 2 was useful because it showed me a simple method I could use in school.

> This is a very good answer as it gives the title, author and publisher of the book and the full URL of the website. It also gives reasons for why each source was useful.

**Repeats (Paper 1)**

3. It is better to repeat each experiment three times. Explain why this is more likely to give a more accurate result.

It is best to do each experiment three times so that I can check my results to see if they are consistent and to look for any anomalous results. I can then calculate mean of my results, leaving out any anomalous results, by adding up the results and dividing by the number of results. This mean will be closer to the true value and reduces the effect of random errors.

> This is a good answer as it describes how you can check that results are consistent, look for anomalous results and then calculate a mean using the remaining results. The answer also explains exactly how the mean is calculated.

# ISA support

## Worked example

**Plan (Paper 1)**

Describe how you plan to do your investigation to test the hypothesis given. You should include:
- the equipment you plan to use
- how you will use the equipment
- the measurements you are going to make
- how you will make it a fair test
- a risk assessment.

You may include a labelled diagram.

### Variables

Independent variable = load on the spring
Dependent variable = extension of spring
Control variable = spring used, temperature

> It is a good idea to state clearly what the independent, dependent and control variables are at the start. This will help you to be clear what you are trying to do.

### Method

1. I will place a spring on a clamp stand. I will place a ruler next to the spring so that the bottom of the spring is next to 0 cm on the ruler.
2. I will add a 100 g slotted mass hanger onto the spring and measure how far the spring stretches, using the ruler.
3. I will keep adding 100 g until I reach 1000 g and measure the extension each time.
4. I will do the experiment three times and find the average of the results.

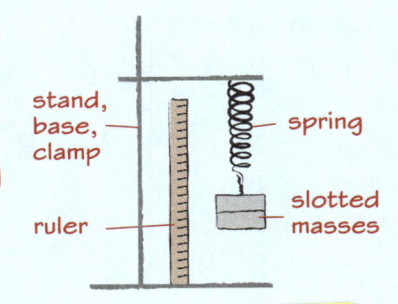

Diagram labels: stand, base, clamp; ruler; spring; slotted masses

> Make sure that you label your diagram.

> Your instructions need to be clear. A good guide is to write the instructions so that someone else in your class could follow them to do your experiment. They need to be written in good English, using full sentences, but they can be numbered. A diagram can be helpful. Use scientific language where it is appropriate.

### Apparatus

Spring, ruler, stand, boss, clamp, slotted mass hanger (100 g), slotted masses (100 g), heavy mass to hold stand down

> It helps to list all the apparatus that you use.

### Fair testing

In order to make this a fair test I must use the same spring each time. I will also make sure the ruler stays in the same place so that the stretch is measured from the same point each time.

> You need to state clearly how you will make the experiment a fair test. You must state which variables you will keep the same.

### Risk assessment:

The main dangers in this experiment are the masses falling off or the stand falling over. I will ensure that the masses are over the bench and not the floor so that they cannot fall on my feet. I will also put a heavy mass on the stand so that it does not topple over.

> You need to identify real risks and suggest ways to prevent these problems happening.

Had a look ☐   Nearly there ☐   Nailed it! ☐   ISA SUPPORT

# ISA support

Paper 2 of the ISA looks at your own results and those from other similar case studies. In many of the questions, it is important to remember to use the data to justify your answers.

The next few examples relate to an experiment where students investigated how changing the distance between a bright lamp and some pondweed affected the number of bubbles of oxygen produced by photosynthesis.

The students' hypothesis was: The closer the lamp is to the pondweed, the greater the rate of photosynthesis (as indicated by more bubbles of oxygen being produced).

The sample questions and comments on this page and the next are all about the experiment with pondweed.

Here are the results recorded by the students.

| Distance from lamp to pondweed cm | Number of bubbles in one minute |
|---|---|
| 10 | 15 |
| 20 | 5 |
| 30 | 3 |
| 40 | 2 |
| 50 | 1 |

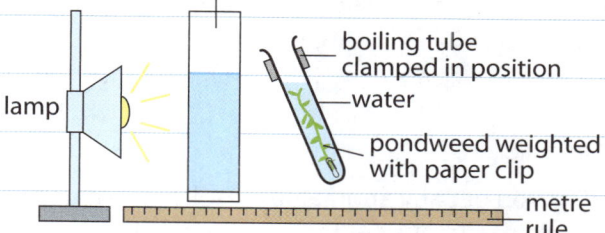

This shows you what the experiment looked like.

Here are the results of some other groups who did the same experiment.

| Distance from lamp to pondweed cm | Number of bubbles in one minute | | |
|---|---|---|---|
| | Group 1 | Group 2 | Group 3 |
| 10 | 20 | 9 | 12 |
| 20 | 10 | 4 | 9 |
| 30 | 4 | 2 | 5 |
| 40 | 2 | 3 | 4 |
| 50 | 1 | 1 | 2 |

## Worked example

**Conclusions (Paper 2)**

What conclusion can you make from your investigation about a link between the distance of the light from the pondweed and the rate of photosynthesis? You should use any pattern that you see in your results to support your conclusion. You should quote some figures from your data to support your answer.

My conclusion is that the closer the lamp is to the pondweed, the greater the rate of photosynthesis. For example, 15 bubbles of oxygen were formed in one minute at 10 cm but only 1 bubble per minute at 50 cm. The effect of the lamp being closer has a bigger difference when you are closer to the pondweed. For example, as the distance is reduced by 10 cm from 30 cm to 20 cm, the number of bubbles per minute increases from 3 to 5, but it increases from 5 to 15 when it is moved from 20 cm to 10 cm.

This is a very good answer. First, it clearly states a conclusion. Second, it uses data from the experiment to support the conclusion. Third, it shows, with data, how the effect becomes greater as the lamp moves closer to the pondweed.

# ISA support

Had a look ☐   Nearly there ☐   Nailed it! ☐

## Worked example

Compare your results with those of others in your class or with your teacher's results. Do you think your results are REPRODUCIBLE? Explain the reasons for your answer.

*Each of the other students' results follows a similar pattern to my own. As the lamp gets closer to the pondweed, there are more bubbles of oxygen in each case. This suggests that the results are quite reproducible. However, although the trend is the same in each case, the actual number of bubbles varies in each case by quite a lot. For example, at 10 cm the results were 20, 9 and 12 bubbles compared to my 15 bubbles per minute.*

> This is a very good answer. It is clear that the student knows that results are reproducible if other students get similar results. The student has commented on the fact that the overall trend is the same, but that the specific results have some variation. The student has also quoted some examples from the data to justify this.

Did you get any anomalous results? Explain your answer. Explain your answer by quoting some data from your investigation.

*I do not believe that I got any anomalous results. All the results fit the overall pattern that as the lamp gets closer to the pondweed, more bubbles of oxygen are formed per minute. Also, all of the measurements lie very close to my best fit line.*

> This is a good answer. It is clear that the student knows that anomalous results are those that do not fit the pattern. It can be hard to answer this question when there are no anomalous results, but the student has commented on the fact that all the results fit the overall pattern and that none of them are far from the best fit line.

What was the independent variable? What was the range? Explain why this was or was not a good range.

*My independent variable is the distance from the lamp to the pondweed. The range was from 10 cm to 50 cm. I believe that this is a good range as it clearly shows the trend that as the distance decreases, the number of bubbles of oxygen per minute increases. It also produces a big difference in the number of bubbles from 15 to 1.*

> This is a good answer. It clearly states the correct variable and range, including units. The answer explains very well why it is a good range.

### Graphs (Paper 2)

You will be awarded up to 4 marks for your chart or graph.

*Here is the graph of my results.*

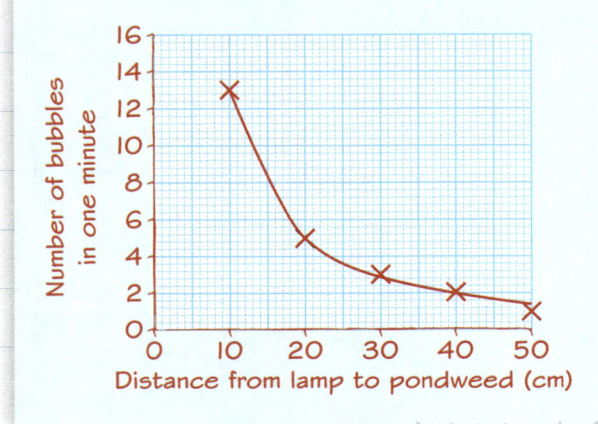

[Graph: Number of bubbles in one minute vs Distance from lamp to pondweed (cm). Curve decreases from about 13 at 10 cm to 1 at 50 cm.]

> You will always have to plot a bar chart or line graph. Plot a bar chart for categoric variables – that is, those that have words, e.g. colours. Plot a line graph for continuous variables – that is, those that are numbers, e.g. temperature. The independent variable should be on the horizontal axis with the dependent variable on the vertical axis.
>
> This is a good graph. The axes have suitable scales. Both axes are labelled and have units. A good best fit line has been plotted that is smooth and has a similar number of points above and below the line. Best fit lines can be straight or curved.

# Answers

You will find some advice next to some of the answers. This is written in italics. It is not part of the mark scheme but just gives you a little more information.

## Biology answers

### 1. Animal and plant cells
1. cell membrane: yes (1); cell wall: yes (1); mitochondria: where respiration takes place releasing energy (1); nucleus: where genes that control the activities of the cell are found (1)
2. Only plant and algal cells can photosynthesise/make their own food (1). Animals don't need chloroplasts because they get their food from eating other organisms (1).

### 2. Different kinds of cells
1. (a) cytoplasm (1)   (b) nucleus (1)
2. A yeast cell has no chloroplasts, unlike a plant cell (1), and it has a cell wall made of different substances than the cell wall of a plant cell (1).
3. The chloroplasts absorb light energy (1), which is used to make food in the plant's cells (1).

### 3. Diffusion
1. B (1)
2. (a) The sum of all movement that is taking place (1).
   (b) The net (overall) movement of particles from a region of their higher concentration to a region of their lower concentration (1).
3. The concentration of particles is higher inside the cell than outside the cell (1). The particles will therefore diffuse down their concentration gradient (1).

### 4. Organisation of the body
1. organ system, organ, tissue, cell (1 mark for all correctly placed)
2. Any two suitable answers, such as: muscular tissue, glandular tissue, epithelial tissue (2). *There are other possible answers, such as skeletal tissue or nervous tissue, but the ones given in the answer above are the ones you will be expected to know.*
3. A tissue is a group of cells with a similar structure and function (1).

### 5. Organs and organ systems
1. tissues (1); muscular tissue/muscle (1)
2. Any two from: salivary glands, pancreas, stomach (2).
3. (a) produces digestive juices and churns the food/where some digestion occurs (1)
   (b) produces bile (1)
   (c) where digestion is completed (1), and soluble food is absorbed (1)

### 6. Plant organs
1. Any one from: stem, root (1). *There are other possible answers, such as a bud or flower, but the ones given in the answer are the ones that you will be expected to know.*
2. Any two from: epidermal tissue, mesophyll tissue, xylem tissue, phloem tissue (2).
3. Appropriate functions for the two answers to Q2, such as: epidermal tissue covers surfaces of the plant; mesophyll tissue carries out photosynthesis; xylem/phloem tissue transport substances around the plant (2).

### 7. Photosynthesis
1. from the soil (1)
2. Any two from: for respiration, to form starch/fat/oil for storage, to make cellulose for cell walls, to produce proteins (2).
3. The nitrate ions are used to change the glucose (sugar) made in photosynthesis (1) into proteins (1).

### 8. Limiting factors
1. Any one from: increasing light intensity, increasing carbon dioxide availability, increasing temperature (1).
2. (a) Oxygen (1), because it is produced by photosynthesising plants (1).
   (b) Light intensity affects the rate of photosynthesis (1). So more oxygen will be produced on the sunny day than on the cloudy day (1).

### 9. Biology six mark question 1
Answers can be found on page 114.

### 10. Distribution of organisms
1. Any two from: amount of light, carbon dioxide availability, oxygen availability, temperature, availability of nutrients, water availability (2).
2. Any two from: high temperature, lack of water, lack of nutrients (2).
3. There is enough light at the edge of the woods for low-growing plants to photosynthesise. (1), Deeper in the wood, the trees shade the ground and there is not enough light for many low-growing plants to photosynthesise. (1).

### 11. Sampling organisms
1. A square frame used to sample organisms in an area (1).
2. Random samples can help to make sure you don't select some types of areas more than others (1). Repeat samples and calculating a mean helps to average out variation that happens by chance (1).
3. 5 + 0 + 2 + 1 + 4 + 3 = 15 (1); mean number = 15/6 = 2.5 daisies (1)

### 12. Transect sampling
1. samples (1); distribution (1)
2. *Enteromorpha* (1), because it is nearest the high water mark/spends most time out of water (1).

### 13. Proteins
1. protein (1)
2. Any two from: structural/for structure in muscle, hormones, antibodies (2). *There are other possible answers, such as haemoglobin, but the ones given in the answer above are the ones you will be expected to know.*
3. The rate of reaction slows down (1) because the temperature affects the shape of the enzyme and it cannot work as well (1).

### 14. Digestive enzymes
1. (a) amylase (1)
   (b) sugars (1)
   (c) Any one from: salivary glands, pancreas, small intestine (1).
2. Digestive enzymes break down large food molecules into smaller molecules (1).

# ANSWERS

## 15. Microbial enzymes
1. Any two from: in biological detergents, in baby food, in slimming foods (2). *Other answers are possible, but the ones given in the answer above are the ones that you are expected to remember.*
2. (a) It changes the shape of the enzyme (1).
   (b) It will slow down the process (1) because the enzyme won't be able to work as well (1).

## 16. Aerobic respiration
1. to build amino acids from sugars, nitrates and other nutrients (1) *There are other possible answers, but the ones given above are the ones you are expected to remember.*
2. mitochondria (1)
3. the breakdown of glucose to release energy (1) using oxygen (1)

## 17. The effect of exercise
1. Any two from: heart rate increases, breathing rate increases, depth of breathing increases (2). *There are other possible answers, but the ones given in the answer above are the ones you are expected to remember.*
2. Oxygen and glucose are needed for respiration to release energy (1). More energy is needed during exercise so that muscles can contract faster (1).
3. Some is stored in the muscle cells as glycogen (1), which is broken down to glucose during exercise (1).

## 18. Anaerobic respiration
1. anaerobic respiration (1)
2. Before point A the muscles can get all the energy they need from aerobic respiration so no lactic acid is produced (1). After point A, the muscles need more and more energy, which is supplied by anaerobic respiration and so lactic acid concentration increases in the blood (1).
3. After vigorous exercise ends, no more lactic acid is produced (1) and blood flow through the muscles takes the lactic acid away (1).

## 19. Biology six mark question 2
Answers can be found on page 114.

## 20. Mitosis
1. Any one from: growth, to replace damaged cells, during asexual reproduction (1).
2. one (1)
3. Body cells are produced by mitosis/all body cells originate from a single fertilised cell (1), where all the genetic material in a cell is copied before it divides to make two new cells (1).

## 21. Sexual reproduction
1. meiosis (1)
2. man/male (1)
3. The egg contains one set of chromosomes/alleles from the mother, and the sperm contains one set of chromosomes/alleles from the father (1). When the egg and sperm join at fertilisation, the new cell has a different mixture of chromosomes/alleles than those in the cells of each parent (1).

## 22. Stem cells
1. bone marrow (1), early embryo (1)
2. A cell that can grow and develop into many different kinds of cell (1).
3. Many plant cells can differentiate into different kinds of specialised cell throughout life (1). Most animal cells differentiate at an early stage and so can only produce more cells of the same kind for replacement and repair (1).

## 23. Genes and alleles
1. (a) iii A large molecule with a double helix structure (1);
   (b) ii A small section of DNA (1)
2. Everybody has a unique DNA fingerprint (except identical twins) (1) so matching a DNA fingerprint with the DNA of a suspect can show that the person was at the scene of the crime (1).

## 24. Genetic diagrams
1. recessive (1)
2. The parent plants both contain one allele for white coloured flowers (1). The parent plants have purple flowers because they have also have an allele for purple-coloured flowers, which is dominant over the allele for white coloured flowers (1). A plant that inherits one allele for white-coloured flowers from each parent will have no dominant allele for purple flowers and so develop white flowers (1).

## 25. Mendel's work
1. Few people read what he had published until after he died (1).
2. Repeats help to average out chance variation (1), which makes the results more reproducible (1).

## 26. Punnett squares
1. polydactyly (1)
2. 2 in 4 (1). *This can be simplified to 1 in 2, or shown as a percentage (50%) or a ratio (1 : 1).*

## 27. Family trees
1. Mia (1)
2. (a) Gill and Harry (1)
   (b) Mia must have inherited one cystic fibrosis allele from each of her parents (1). But neither Gill nor Harry have the disease so they must have one cystic fibrosis allele and one allele that doesn't cause cystic fibrosis (1). *Other descendants of Arun and Beth could also be carriers, but we can't work this out from the information in the diagram, so they would not be marked correct.*

## 28. Embryo screening
1. screening (1); inherited (1)
2. There is a chance of the embryo inheriting two alleles for the disorder from the parents and so suffering from cystic fibrosis (1). Screening of the embryo gives parents the choice to terminate an embryo that will develop the disease (1).

## 29. Fossils
1. traces or remains of organisms in rocks from many years ago (1)
2. (a) Soft-bodied animals don't form fossils as easily as the bones of vertebrates (1). *You could also say that soft parts of organisms/soft bodies are more likely to rot or be eaten before they can form fossils.*
   (b) Any one from: geological activity destroys fossils, so removing evidence of evolution (1); fossils only form in special conditions so there may not be fossils of many species. (1)

## 30. Extinction
1. B (1). *There is evidence that an asteroid hit Earth 65 million years ago, but many types of dinosaur were already extinct by then. So it is not correct to say that 'all dinosaurs' were killed by the asteroid*
2. Any two suitable reasons, such as: all the individuals of a species may have been killed for food by humans or rats (1); the rats may have eaten all the prey of some of the animals, so they had no food and died (1).

# ANSWERS

### 31. Biology six mark question 3
Answers can be found on page 114–5.

# Chemistry answers

### 32. Forming ions
1. (a) The bromine atom gains one electron in its outer shell **(1)**.
   (b) The magnesium atom loses its two outer electrons **(1)**.
2. Diagram completed correctly to show eight electrons in their highest occupied energy level (outer shell) **(1)**.

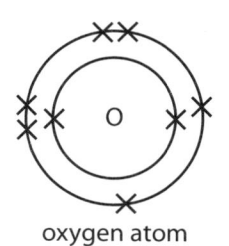

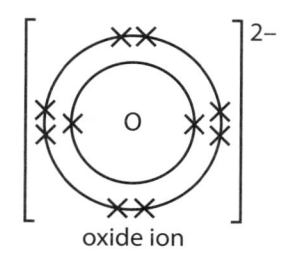

   oxygen atom    oxide ion

3. The charge would be 3– **(1)** because atoms from Group 5 need to gain three electrons to have a noble gas structure (or to fill their outer shell) **(1)**.

### 33. Ionic compounds
1. (a) copper(II) (or copper) and chloride (both needed for the mark) **(1)**
   (b) two **(1)**
2. (a) Diagram completed with correct numbers of electrons *Electrons can be shown as crosses or dots.* **(1)**; brackets around the diagram with a minus sign for the charge **(1)**.

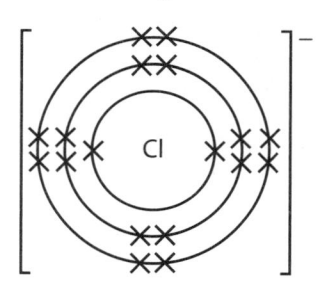

   (b) The chlorine atom gains one electron in its highest occupied energy level (outer shell) **(1)**.
   (c) $MgCl_2$ **(1)**
3. $Na_2O$ **(1)**

### 34. Giant ionic structures
1. Sodium ions have a single positive charge and chloride ions have a single negative charge **(1)**; the oppositely charged ions attract each other **(1)**.
2. A (strong) electrostatic force of attraction **(1)** between oppositely charged ions **(1)**.
3. (a) Diagram completed with correct numbers of electrons (shown as crosses or dots) **(1)**; brackets around the diagram with a 2– sign for the charge **(1)**.

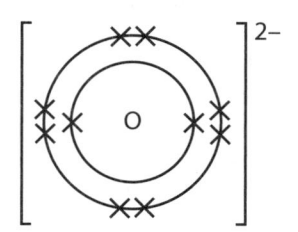

   (b) Diagram completed with correct numbers of electrons (shown as crosses or dots) **(1)**; brackets around the diagram with a 2+ sign for the charge **(1)**.

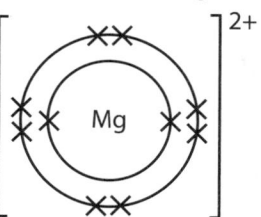

   (c) A magnesium ion forms when a magnesium atom loses two electrons **(1)**, but an oxide ion forms when an oxygen atom gains two electrons **(1)**.

### 35. Covalent bonds in simple molecules
1. a shared pair of electrons **(1)**
2. Diagram with five overlapping circles **(1)**, with a dot and a cross inside each overlapping area **(1)** and the correct element symbols inside **(1)**.

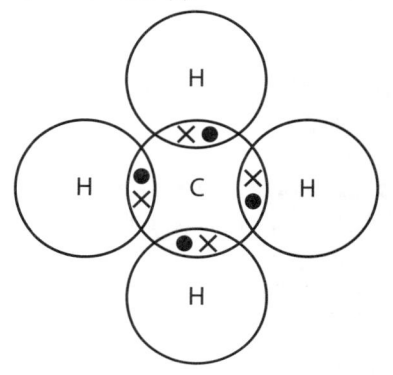

### 36. Covalent bonds in macromolecules
1. covalent bonding **(1)**
2. Diagram B shows the macromolecule **(1)** because it contains many atoms (or A only contains 5 atoms) **(1)**.

### 37. Properties of molecules
1. (a) all **(1)**
   (b) four **(1)**
2. (a) three **(1)**
   (b) covalent **(1)**

### 38. Properties of ionic compounds
1. strong ionic **(1)**
2. (a) Melt it to form a liquid **(1)** because then the ions will be free to move around **(1)** and carry the current.
   (b) Aluminium oxide is an ionic compound so it will have a high melting point **(1)** and a lot of energy will be needed to melt it **(1)**, which could be expensive.

### 39. Metals
1. (a) a mixture of two or more metals (or a mixture of a metal and at least one other element) **(1)**
   (b) in a giant structure **(1)** with the atoms regularly arranged in layers **(1)**
2. (a) Advantage: The metal should be very strong (stronger than the metals in the table) **(1)**. Disadvantage: The metal is more likely to crack **(1)**.
   (b) Adding carbon increases the strength of the metal **(1)** because its atoms disrupt the layers **(1)** making it more difficult for the layers of iron atoms to slide over each other **(1)**.

# ANSWERS

### 40. Polymers
1. It melts/softens (1).
2. It has cross-links (1).
3. LDPE would be best (1) because although it is not as strong as HDPE (1) it is more flexible (1). *Note that the highest useful temperature does not matter for this use.*

### 41. Nanoscience
1. hundred atoms (1)
2. (a) Nanoparticles are only 1–100 nm in size (1), which is too small to see (1).
   (b) Any two advantages for one mark each: the building stays warmer in winter, the building stays cooler in summer, reduced energy costs, reduced use of fossil fuels, reduced carbon dioxide emissions (2).

### 42. Different structures
1. simple molecular (1)
2. (a) giant covalent/macromolecular (1)
   (b) graphite (1)

### 43. Chemistry six mark question 1
Answers can be found on page 115.

### 44. Atomic structure and isotopes
1. Second and third boxes ticked for one mark each (2).
2. All three atoms have one proton (1) and so are all hydrogen (1), but they have different numbers of neutrons (1): $^1_1H$ has none, $^2_1H$ has one, and $^3_1H$ has two (1).

### 45. Relative formula mass
1. (a) $16 + 16 = 32$ OR $(2 \times 16) = 32$ (1)
   (b) $12 + 16 + 16 = 44$ OR $12 + (16 \times 16) = 44$ (1)
   (c) $23 + 1 + 16 = 40$ (1)
2. (a) $(2 \times 23) + 12 + (3 \times 16) = 46 + 12 + 48 = 106$ (1)
   (b) $24 + 32 + (4 \times 16) = 56 + 64 = 120$ (1)
   (c) $(2 \times 12) + (6 \times 1) = 24 + 6 = 30$ (1)

### 46. Paper chromatography
1. (a) two (1)
   (b) colours B and C (1)
2. (a) Pencil does not dissolve/ink from the pen would dissolve in the solvent (1).
   (b) The lid stops the solvent evaporating (1).

### 47. Gas chromatography
1. (a) separates them (1)
   (b) the number of different substances in the sample (1)
   (c) the time taken for the substance to pass through the column to the detector (1)
   (d) identifies substances (1) *'Gives the $M_r$ of a substance' is also an acceptable answer.*
   (e) gas chromatography linked to mass spectroscopy (1)

### 48. Percentage composition
1. $M_r$ of $CH_4 = 16$ (1) % of C in $CH_4 = \frac{12}{16} \times 100\%$ (1) $= 75\%$ (1)
2. $M_r$ of $NH_3 = 17$ (1) % of N in $NH_3 = \frac{14}{17} \times 100\%$ (1) $= 82.4\%$ (1)
3. $M_r$ of $CO_2 = 44$ (1) % of O in $CO_2$. $= \frac{(2 \times 16)}{44} \times 100\%$ (1) $= 72.7\%$ (1)
4. $M_r$ of $NH_4NO_3 = 80$ (1) % of N in $NH_4NO_3$
   $= \frac{(2 \times 14)}{80} \times 100\%$ (1) $= 35\%$ (1)

### 49. Reaction yields
1. the amount of product obtained (1)
2. (a) The actual yield is usually less (1).
   (b) Any two reasons for one mark each: the reaction does not go to completion, some product may be lost during separation (such as filtration), other reactions may happen as well (leading to by-products) (2).

### 50. Reversible reactions
1. The reaction is reversible (1).
2. Add water (1) and observe a colour change from white to blue (1).

### 51. Rates of reaction
1. measuring the amount of reactant used over time (1), measuring the amount of product formed over time (1)
2. Any two of the following for 1 mark each: the rate of reaction is fast at first/then slows down/until it stops (2).
3. (a) 90 seconds (1) (this is where the graph first levels off)
   (b) 90 cm³ (1) (this is the maximum volume formed)
   (c) $90/90 = 1$ cm³/s (1 mark for the correct answer, 1 mark for the correct unit)

### 52. Changing rates 1
1. First and third boxes ticked for one mark each (2).
2. Increasing the temperature increases the rate of reaction (1) because the particles move faster (1) so they collide more frequently (1) and with more energy (1).

### 53. Changing rates 2
1. increase the pressure (1), increase the temperature (1), add a catalyst (1)
2. (a) It is a catalyst (1), which increases the rate of reaction (1) and so reduces costs (1).
   (b) for using a high temperature: faster rate of reaction (1); against using a high temperature – one of the following for one mark: higher energy cost/the oils could go off or break down/the oils could catch fire (1)
3. Concentrated acid contains more reactant particles in the same volume (1), so the frequency of collisions with magnesium particles is increased (1).

### 54. Chemistry six mark question 2
Answers can be found on page 115.

### 55. Energy changes
1. a process that gives out (1) heat/energy to the surroundings (1)
2. It is endothermic (1) because energy is taken in from the surroundings/the electricity transfers energy to the water (1).
3. The reaction to produce anhydrous copper sulfate is endothermic (1). *You can tell this because the reactants have to be continuously heated.* As it is a reversible reaction, the other reaction must be exothermic (1), so it gives out heat energy to the surroundings (1).

### 56. Acids and alkalis
1. (a) a substance (metal oxide or metal hydroxide) that can neutralise acids (1)
   (b) a soluble hydroxide/base (1)
2. (a) hydrogen ions, $H^+(aq)$ (1); (b) hydroxide ions, $OH^-(aq)$ (1)
3. (a) a substance that changes colour depending on its pH (1)
   (b) Phenolphthalein will be colourless (1) because acids are below pH 7 (1). *Note that 'clear' is not the same as colourless and is not correct.*

# ANSWERS

4. Hydrogen ions from the acid **(1)** react with hydroxide ions from the alkali **(1)**; H$^+$(aq) + OH$^-$(aq) → H$_2$O(l) (**1** mark for correct formulae with the ions in either order, **1** mark for correct state symbols).

## 57. Making salts
1. (a) potassium chloride **(1)**
   (b) sodium nitrate **(1)**
   (c) ammonium sulfate **(1)** *Note that ammonia sulfate is incorrect.*
2. Use hydrochloric acid **(1)** and sodium hydroxide **(1)**; add an indicator to some alkali and add acid until it changes colour **(1)**; then evaporate the water **(1)**.

## 58. Making soluble salts
1. Potassium is too reactive/it would be dangerous to add potassium to acid **(1)**.
2. (a) One from the following for one mark: zinc, zinc oxide, zinc hydroxide **(1)**.
   (b) Add excess solid to hydrochloric acid **(1)**, filter **(1)** and evaporate **(1)**.
3. (a) nitric acid **(1)**, magnesium oxide/magnesium hydroxide **(1)**
   (b) magnesium oxide + nitric acid → magnesium nitrate + water (all four needed for 1 mark; magnesium hydroxide instead of magnesium oxide is acceptable) **(1)**

## 59. Making insoluble salts
1. (a) Solutions react together to make an insoluble salt **(1)**.
   (b) CdCO$_3$ **(1)**; because it is a solid/it has the state symbol (s) **(1)**.
2. A soluble calcium compound for one mark, e.g. calcium nitrate, calcium chloride (not calcium hydroxide) **(1)**; a soluble carbonate for one mark, e.g. sodium carbonate, ammonium carbonate **(1)**.

## 60. Using electricity
1. The negative electrode **(1)** because opposite charges attract **(1)**.
2. The ions are able to move about in molten lead bromide **(1)** but not in solid lead bromide **(1)**.
3. The positive electrode should be made of copper **(1)**, the negative electrode should be the machine parts **(1)**, the electrolyte should be a solution containing copper ions **(1)** such as copper sulfate/copper nitrate/copper chloride **(1)**.

## 61. Useful substances from electrolysis
1. Electricity is expensive/positive electrodes must be replaced often/aluminium oxide must be melted **(1)**.
2. Aluminium oxide dissolves in molten cryolite **(1)** at a lower temperature than the melting point of aluminium oxide **(1)** (which reduces energy costs).
3. Hydrogen is formed at the negative electrode **(1)**; chlorine is formed at the positive electrode **(1)** because hydrogen ions are positive and chloride ions are negative **(1)** and opposite charges attract **(1)**.

## 62. Electrolysis products
1. hydrogen ions **(1)** and hydroxide ions **(1)** from water **(1)**
2. During the electrolysis of potassium hydroxide solution, hydrogen is produced at the negative electrode **(1)** because hydrogen ions are present **(1)** and potassium is more reactive than hydrogen **(1)**; during the electrolysis of molten potassium hydroxide, potassium is produced at the negative electrode **(1)** (because there are no hydrogen ions).

## 63. Chemistry six mark question 3
Answers can be found on page 115.

# Physics answers

## 64. Resultant forces
1. 12 N **(1)** upwards **(1)**
2. (a) 80 N + 60 N **(1)** = 140 N **(1)**
   (b) The car accelerates or starts to move **(1)** forwards **(1)**
3. (a) 25 N − 15 N − 10 N **(1)** = 0 N **(1)**
   (b) The bicycle moves at a constant speed or its speed/velocity does not change **(1)**.

## 65. Forces and motion
1. (a) 5 kg/20 N **(1)** = 4 m/s$^2$ **(1)**
   (b) Moving at a steady speed **(1)** in the direction of the force **(1)**
2. $a$ = 400 N/3200 kg **(1)** = 0.125 **(1)** m/s$^2$ **(1)**
3. (a) F = 0.16 kg × −10 m/s$^2$ **(1)** = −1.6 N **(1)** *The answer must include the minus sign.*
   (b) The ball slows down/decelerates **(1)** because the force is negative/acting downwards **(1)**.

## 66. Distance–time graphs
1. (a) graph with $y$-axis labelled 'distance in m' and $x$-axis labelled 'time in s' with suitable scales **(1)**; all 5 points plotted correctly **(2)**; straight line drawn through all five points **(1)**
   (b) straight line starting from the origin **(1)** with a steeper gradient than A **(1)**
   (c) horizontal line **(1)** at 5 m from the origin **(1)**

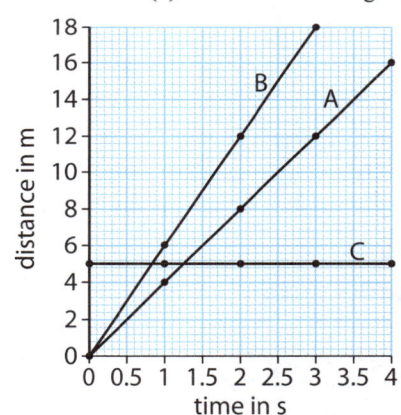

## 67. Acceleration and velocity
1. (a) accelerating **(1)**
   (b) has a larger acceleration **(1)**
   (c) moving at a constant velocity **(1)**
2. $a = \dfrac{80 \text{ m/s} - 0 \text{ m/s}}{40 \text{ s}}$ **(1)** = 2 **(1)** m/s$^2$

## 68. Forces and braking
1. Stopping distance = 9 m + 14 m **(1)** = 23 m **(1)**; this is less than the distance to the child **(1)**.
2. The kinetic energy is reduced **(1)** because it is transferred and increases the temperature of the cycle brakes and/or the surroundings **(1)**.
3. The F1 driver has a shorter thinking distance because he/she is better trained/more alert/less tired **(1)**; the F1 braking distance is shorter because the braking force is greater or the tyres are less worn/produce more friction with the road, or the racetrack is not as smooth/slippery as the road **(1)**.

# ANSWERS

## 69. Falling objects

1. W = 62 kg × 10 N/kg **(1)** = 620 **(1)** N **(1)**

| Stage of the fall | Weight greater than resistance | Weight equals resistance | Resistance greater than weight |
|---|---|---|---|
| He steps out of the capsule. | ✓ **(1)** | | |
| He is falling at a constant velocity. | | ✓ **(1)** | |
| He opens his parachute. | | | ✓ **(1)** |
| He is falling at a constant velocity of a few metres/second. | | ✓ **(1)** | |

## 70. Forces and terminal velocity

1. (a) C/D and E/F **(1)** (both needed for one mark)
   (b) A to C **(1)** (AB and BC)
   (c) D/E **(1)**
2. axes drawn with an appropriate scale **(1)**; line with positive gradient (*straight or curved*) drawn from origin to 20 m/s at 3 s **(1)**; horizontal line at 20 m/s for 3 to 6 s **(1)**

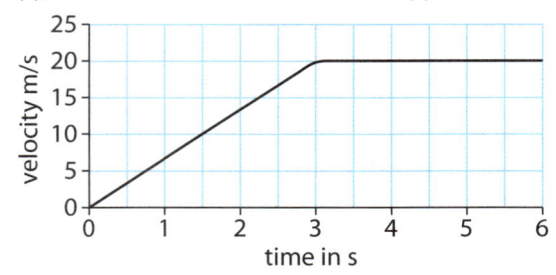

## 71. Elasticity

1. (a) stretched **(1)**
   (b) regains its original shape **(1)**
   (c) gets larger **(1)**
2. extension = 54 − 50 = 4 m **(1)**; $F$ = 230 N/m × 4 m **(1)** = 920 N **(1)**

## 72. Forces and energy

1. (a) energy transferred = work done = force × distance **(1)**
       80 N × 4 m **(1)** = 320 J **(1)**
   (b) $P$ = 320 J/2 s **(1)** = 160 W **(1)**
2. The frictional/resistive force of the air **(1)** does work. The kinetic energy of the meteorite is transferred into raising the temperature of the meteorite (and the air) **(1)**.

## 73. KE and GPE

1. $E_p$ = 70 kg × 10 N/kg × 3 m **(1)** = 2100 J **(1)**
2. $E_k = \frac{1}{2}$ × 200 kg × (373 m/s)$^2$ **(1)** = 13 912 900 J **(1)** (or about 14 MJ)

## 74. Momentum

1. The truck has the larger momentum **(1)** because it has the larger mass **(1)**.
2. (a) moving carriage, $p$ = 0.2 kg × 0.8 m/s **(1)** = 0.16 kg m/s, stationary carriage $p$ = 0 **(1)**;
       so total momentum = 0.16 kg m/s **(1)**
   (b) It is a closed system/nothing is added or taken away **(1)** so momentum is conserved **(1)**.
   (c) The joined up carriages move in the same direction as the moving carriage was moving **(1)** because the momentum is 0.16 kg m/s in the same direction **(1)**.

## 75. Physics six mark question 1

Answers can be found on page 115–6.

## 76. Static electricity

1. The rods will be attracted to each other. **(1)**
2. Some clothes gain electrons and some lose electrons **(1)**; the clothes have opposite electrical charges **(1)**; opposite electrical charges attract **(1)**.

## 77. Current and potential difference

1. work done – joules **(1)**, electric current – amperes **(1)**, electric charge – coulombs **(1)**, potential difference – volts **(1)**
2. (a) $V$ = 90 J/12 C **(1)** = 7.5 V **(1)**
   (b) $I$ = 12 C/5 s **(1)** = 2.4 A **(1)**

## 78. Circuit diagrams

1. (a) C **(1)**
   (b) C has a cell/source of electrical energy, A does not **(1)**, C has no breaks in the circuit/the switch is closed, the circuit in B is broken/the switch is open **(1)**
2. Complete circuit using the correct symbols (**1 mark for each correct symbol, 1 mark for all linked together without breaks. Parallel arrangements are allowed**).

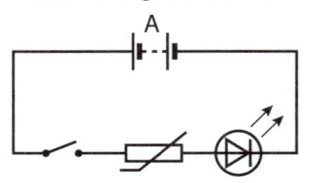

## 79. Resistors

1. (a) 3 **(1)** A or amperes **(1)**
   (b) −3 **(1)** V or volts **(1)**
2. (a) Resistor Q has double the resistance of Resistor P **(2)** (**1** mark for simply stating that the resistance of Q is larger than P).
   (b) 3 V **(2)**

## 80. Series and parallel

1. (a) Correct symbols for components **(1)** arranged in a complete series circuit **(1)**. 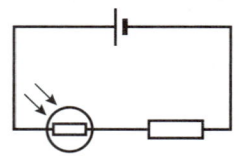
   (b) Correct symbols for components **(1)** arranged in a parallel circuit **(1)**. 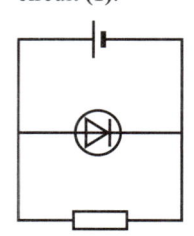
2. 6 cells **(1)** in series **(1)**

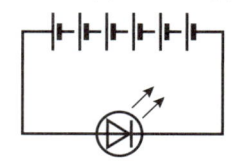

3. In a series circuit the same current flows through both lamps (1), so if one breaks the circuit is broken and no current flows (1). In a parallel circuit if one bulb breaks the current can continue to flow through the unbroken circuit, which includes the unbroken lamp (1).

## 81. Variable resistance

1. In the dark the resistance of the LDR is high so the current is too low to light the LED (1).
2. When cold the resistance of the thermistor is high/ the current is low (1) and the LED not lit (1). When the motor is hot the resistance of the thermistor falls/current rises (1) and the LED lights up (1).

## 82. Using electrical circuits

1. (a) total current = 10 × 0.03 A (1) = 0.3 A (1)
   (b) V = 0.03 A × 200 Ω (1) = 6 V (1)
   (c) 6 V (1)
2. Any three points from: The filament lamp takes a lot more current from the battery (1), so more charge flows every second (1), and more energy is supplied by the battery every second (1). The filament lamp uses up the energy of the cell more quickly (1). The battery will have to be replaced more often with the filament lamp/the filament lamp wastes more energy than the LEDs (1).

## 83. Different currents

1. In a.c. the current changes direction regularly, in d.c it has a fixed direction (1). Mains electricity has higher potential difference than cells (1).
2. Batteries are portable/can be used anywhere (1). Mains supply does not run out (1) OR Mains electricity is cheaper than batteries (1) OR Mains is used to run more powerful appliances (1).
3. twice (1)

## 84. Three-pin plugs

1. (a) (i) blue (1) (ii) green and yellow (stripes) (1)
   (b) the earth pin (1)
2. Two from: The wires in the cables have two layers of insulation (1). The casing of the plug is made of plastic/an insulating material (1). The plug has a cable grip to prevent the wires from being pulled out (1).

## 85. Electrical safety

1. (a) 13 A (1),  (b) 3 A (1),  (c) 13 A (1)
2. 3 core cable contains an earth lead (1). If a fault makes the metal case carry a current the earth lead will conduct the current away (1) (and blow the fuse) OR a two-core cable does not contain an earth lead (1) so a fault resulting in a current in the metal case will give a shock (1).

## 86. Current and power

1. (a) P = 0.1 A × 230 V (1) = 23 W (1)
   (b) The CFL uses less power than the filament lamp but gives out the same amount of light energy (1), so the filament lamp must transfer more/the CFL must transfer less electrical energy to heat the surroundings (1).
2. (a) power = current × potential difference
           = 8.7 A × 230 V (1)
           = 2001 W, or 2 kW (1)
   (b) The current is more than 3 A but less than 13A (1) so a 13A fuse is necessary (1).

## 87. Physics six mark question 2

Answers can be found on page 116.

## 88. Atomic structure

1. (a) protons and neutrons (1)
   (b) protons and electrons (1)
   (c) electrons (1)
2. (a) protons – 3 (1), neutrons – 4 (1), electrons – 3 (1)
   (b) Like atoms of X, Y has 3 protons and 4 neutrons/it has the same mass number (1), but Y only has 2 electrons (1).

## 89. Background radiation

1. (a) Any one from: radon gas, cosmic rays, food and drinks, buildings (1)
   (b) Any one from: medical, nuclear power, nuclear weapons tests (1).
2. (a) Radioactive decay is random (1).
   (b) Their dose of radiation is higher (1) because the amount/concentration of radon gas in the air is higher underground (1).

## 90. Alpha, beta and gamma radiation

1. (a) alpha (1); (b) gamma (1); (c) beta (1)
2. Alpha is more ionising than beta (1); alpha is less penetrating than beta OR alpha is stopped by a sheet of paper/few cm of air but beta is not (1); alpha is positively charged, beta is negative OR alpha is deflected towards negative charges, beta to positive (1).

## 91. Half-life

1. The activity has fallen to one quarter of its starting value (1) because two periods of half-life have passed (1).
2. (a) 80/2 = 40, 40/2 = 20, so two periods of half-life have passed (1); 2 × half-life = 12 hours. So half-life is 12/2 = 6 hours (1).
   (b) This is suitable because it allows time for the sample to reach the cancers and for the radiation to be detected (1), but in a short time/a day there will be almost no radioactivity left in the patient (1).

## 92. Uses and dangers

1. alpha – smoke alarms (1); beta – checking cardboard cartons (1); gamma – finding leaks (1)
2. Gamma is the only type of radiation that will travel through the body to be detected (1). Gamma is the least ionising type of radiation so will cause the least damage to healthy cells (1).

## 93. The nuclear model of the atom

1. B (1)
2. The nuclear atom explained the evidence better than the plum pudding model (1) because it shows that the atom is largely empty space with the mass and positive charge concentrated in the nucleus (1).

## 94. Nuclear fission

1. B (1)
2. A diagram showing neutron hitting U-235 nucleus (1); 2 or 3 neutrons formed (and fission products) (1); one neutron going on to hit another U-235 nucleus (1).

## 95. Nuclear fusion

1. D: iron (1)
2. (a) Elements heavier than hydrogen are formed by nuclear fusion reactions (1) in stars (1).
   (b) Heavy elements (like gold and uranium) are formed in nuclear fusion reactions (1) when a star explodes as a supernova (1).

# ANSWERS

### 96. The lifecycle of stars

1. protostar → main sequence stars → red giant → white dwarf → black dwarf (all correct, **(3)**; 4 in correct order, **(2)**; 3 in correct order, **(1)**
2. Stars have so much matter **(1)** the fusion reactions of hydrogen and heavier elements **(1)** can last billions of years. *The answer should refer to the size of stars and that there are many different fusion reactions that produce heavier elements, up to iron.*

### 97. Physics six mark question 3

Answers can be found on page 116.

## Six mark question answers

A basic answer is usually badly organised, has only basic information in it, does not use scientific words and includes poor spelling, punctuation and grammar.

A good answer usually contains accurate information and shows a clear understanding of the subject. The answer will have some structure and the candidate will have tried to use some scientific words, but it might not always be accurate and there may not be all the detail needed to answer the question. There will be a few errors with spelling, punctuation and grammar.

An excellent answer contains accurate information, is detailed and is supported by relevant examples. The answer will be well organised and will contain lots of relevant scientific words that are used in the correct way. The spelling, punctuation and grammar will be almost faultless.

### 9. Biology six mark question 1

A basic answer will give at least one example of a cell, tissue and organ within the digestive system but little attempt to describe their functions.

A good answer will give at least one example of a cell, tissue and organ within the digestive system, showing some understanding of what their functions are. An attempt may be shown of how this relates to the function of the digestive system as a whole.

An excellent answer will include a clear, well-organised and detailed explanation of the functions of a range of tissues and organs in the digestive system, and what the overall function of the digestive system is.

Examples of points made in the response:
- Differentiated cells with similar function are organised into tissues.
- Tissues are organised into organs.
- Organs in the digestive system work together to carry out the functions of digesting food and absorbing soluble food into the body.

Examples of cells:
- muscle cells in muscular tissue
- glandular cells in glandular/secretory tissue
- epithelial cells in epithelial tissue.

Examples of tissues:
- muscular tissue that contracts and so churns food in the stomach
- glandular cells that secrete digestive juices into the digestive system to digest food
- epithelial tissue covers the surfaces of the organs in the digestive system.

Examples of organs:
- stomach where digestion is carried out
- pancreas and salivary glands that produce digestive juices
- liver, which produces bile
- small intestine where digestion is completed and soluble food is absorbed
- large intestine where water is absorbed, leaving faeces.

### 19. Biology six mark question 2

A basic answer will give a brief description of one change that occurs during exercise, with an attempt to link a high level of exercise to a high level of heart rate/breathing rate/depth of breathing.

A good answer will give a description and explanation of at least two changes that occur during exercise, with clear indication that the changes increase as the level of exercise increases. Reference to aerobic and anaerobic respiration should be made.

An excellent answer will include a clear, balanced and detailed description and explanation of the changes that happen in the body as a result of increasing exercise. This should be linked to the rate of aerobic respiration increasing to release more energy for muscle contraction. Reference should be made to the role of anaerobic respiration in delivering additional energy when exercise is very vigorous.

Examples of points made in the response:
- heart rate increases as exercise level increases to pump blood faster around the body
- breathing rate and depth of breathing increase as exercise level increases to exchange oxygen and carbon dioxide more rapidly with the environment
- blood delivers oxygen and glucose to muscle cells more rapidly, and removes carbon dioxide rapidly
- muscles cells need more oxygen and glucose for faster aerobic respiration to release energy more rapidly so the muscles can contract faster or more strongly
- increasing amounts of carbon dioxide are produced as a result of respiration
- carbon dioxide is removed to prevent build-up of carbon dioxide in cells, which could affect enzymes and so affect other reactions
- if exercise is very vigorous aerobic respiration cannot deliver all the energy that muscle cells need for contracting
- when aerobic respiration cannot supply enough oxygen, then anaerobic respiration supplies additional energy
- energy is released in anaerobic respiration from the breakdown of glucose to lactic acid without the use of oxygen.

### 31. Biology six mark question 3

A basic answer will give a brief explanation of one fact about fossil formation, such as soft-bodied organisms don't form fossils easily, or one possible reason for extinction.

A good answer will give a good explanation including a detailed description about how soft-bodied organisms form fossils or a detailed explanation of how organisms may become extinct, or a brief explanation of how fossils are formed and a brief explanation of how species may become extinct.

An excellent answer will include a clear, balanced and detailed explanation of the formation of fossils by soft-bodied organisms and a range of possible reasons for their extinction from the fossil record including geological activity.

Examples of points made in the response:
How fossils form:
- A fossil is evidence of organisms that lived a long time ago.
- Fossils of soft-bodied organisms only form in very special conditions before the soft tissue decays/usually only hard parts of an organism fossilise.
- Fossils may be formed as other materials replace decaying tissue.
- Soft-bodied organisms also leave trace fossils such as burrows.

Why the fossil record is not complete:
- Reason for disappearance from fossil record may be that rocks containing the fossils have been destroyed by geological activity
- or that the special conditions in which they formed never happened again
- or they became extinct because the more recent organisms were predators that ate them all
- or more recent organisms were able to outcompete them for resources
- or more recent organisms brought diseases that killed them all
- or the Ediacaran fossils evolved into the more recent species so it only looks like they disappear from the fossil record.

## 43. Chemistry six mark question 1

A basic answer will contain a simple description of one or more reasons why the alloy is used. Little information from the table is used.

A good answer will give a clear explanation of some reasons why the alloy is used. Information from the table and scientific knowledge is used in support.

An excellent answer will contain a clear, balanced and detailed explanation of several reasons why the alloy is used. These are fully supported using information from the table and scientific knowledge.

Examples of points made in the response:

Information from the table:
- The alloy has a (2.8 times) lower density than steel.
- Aircraft parts made from the alloy will be lighter than the same parts made from steel.
- Lighter parts will save on fuel (or another advantage, such as ability to fly).
- The alloy is (4.7 times) stronger than aluminium alone.
- The alloy is (2.5 times) weaker than steel.
- The alloy has a better strength to weight ratio than steel (1.7 compared with 1.5).

Information from prior knowledge:
- Aluminium is a metal.
- Layers of atoms in metals can slide over each other.
- Metals can be bent and shaped.
- Different-sized atoms in alloys make it more difficult for layers to slide over each other.
- Aluminium alloy should be harder than aluminium alone.
- Aluminium does not corrode easily (but steel does).

## 54. Chemistry six mark question 2

A basic answer includes a brief description of either an advantage or a disadvantage of using each process.

A good answer includes a brief advantage and disadvantage of using each process or a good explanation of either the advantages or disadvantages of one process. Information from the descriptions is used in support of the answer.

An excellent answer includes a clear, balanced and detailed description of the advantages and disadvantages of each process and comes to appropriate conclusion, fully supported by relevant knowledge and information from the descriptions.

Examples of points made in the response:

Advantages of Process 1:
- More energy is released per gram of magnesium.
- The packaging may be lighter if less reactant is needed.

Disadvantages of Process 1:
- Hydrogen is produced, which is flammable.
- Magnesium hydroxide is produced, which is alkaline (and so harmful).

Advantages of Process 2:
- No other substance is produced.
- Calcium chloride is a salt (and so safer).

Disadvantages of Process 2:
- Less energy is produced per gram of calcium chloride.
- The packaging may be heavier if more reactant is needed.

Other points:
- The rate of reaction is not given, so one process may heat the food up faster than the other.
- The volume or mass of water needed for each process is not given.
- One process may need larger cans than the other process to contain the reactants.

## 63. Chemistry six mark question 3

A basic answer will include a few brief points covering how aluminium is extracted by the electrolysis of aluminium oxide.

A good answer will include a good description of how aluminium is extracted by the electrolysis of aluminium oxide.

An excellent answer will give a clear, balanced and detailed description of how aluminium is extracted by the electrolysis of aluminium oxide.

Examples of points made in the response:
- Aluminium oxide is dissolved/molten.
- The ions are free to move in the molten cryolite.
- The use of cryolite reduces the temperature needed for the process.
- Aluminium ions are attracted to the negative electrode.
- Aluminium ions gain electrons/form aluminium atoms at the negative electrode.
- Oxide ions are attracted to the positive electrode.
- Oxide ions lose electrons/form oxygen gas at the positive electrode.
- Oxygen reacts with carbon at the positive electrode, forming carbon dioxide.

## 75. Physics six mark question 1

A basic answer will include a brief reference to thinking or braking distance contributing to stopping distance or factors that affect either thinking and/or braking distance.

A good answer will include some explanation of factors that affect both thinking and braking distance, and that these factors change the overall stopping distance of the vehicle.

An excellent answer will include a clear, balanced and detailed explanation of how a number of factors affect thinking and braking distance and the overall stopping distance.

Examples of points made in the response:
- Stopping distance is the sum of thinking distance and braking distance.
- Thinking distance is the distance covered by the vehicle while the driver reacts to the event.
- Braking distance is the distance travelled while the force of the brakes acting decreases the velocity of the vehicle.
- Stopping distance increases with the speed of the vehicle (that is, both thinking and braking distances increase with increasing speed).
- Thinking distance can be increased if the driver is slower to react because they are:
  - tired
  - affected by alcohol or drugs
  - distracted, e.g. by conversation with a passenger or mobile phone.

# ANSWERS

- Braking distance can be increased if:
  - the tyres on the car are worn smooth so there is less friction with the road
  - the brakes/brake pads are worn so there is less friction on the wheels
  - the road is wet or icy or its surface is slippery, reducing the friction of the tyres with the road
  - the vehicle is heavier, because heavier vehicles have a greater momentum so need a greater braking force or increased braking distance.

## 87. Physics six mark question 2

A basic answer will include a brief description of the different properties of LEDs or filament lamps.

A good answer will include a brief description of the properties of filament lamps and LEDs or a more detailed description of either filament lamps or LEDs. There may also be a comment on reasons why LEDs are replacing filament lamps.

An excellent answer will include clear, balanced and detailed description of the current/voltage characteristics of filament lamps and LEDs as well as a well-argued explanation for why LEDs are replacing filament lamps.

Examples of points made in the response:
- Filament lamps contain a wire that glows when a current passes through it.
- The resistance of a filament lamp increases with voltage or the increase in current flowing decreases with increasing voltage.
- Filament lamps dissipate more electrical energy as waste energy than LEDs – the waste energy heats the surroundings.
- Filament lamps are very inefficient/have a very low efficiency.
- Efficiency is useful energy output/energy input.
- LEDs are light-emitting diodes.
- LEDs are semiconductor devices.
- LEDs only conduct electricity in one direction.
- Above a threshold voltage they show a steady increase in current with voltage.
- Very little of the energy used by an LED is wasted.
- LEDs have a high efficiency.
- For the same light output the cost of electricity supplied to LEDs is much lower than for filament lamps.
- The lower running costs of LEDs outweigh the higher initial/purchase costs. Using LEDs reduces waste of electricity/saves electricity/reduces use of fossil fuels.
- Filament lamps are being phased out so are getting difficult to purchase. People are having to buy low-energy lamps.

## 97. Physics six mark question 3

A basic answer will include a brief outline of the danger of radiation or a property of one type of radiation or a safety precaution.

A good answer will include some comparison of the hazards of all three types of radiation and may contain some safety precautions.

An excellent answer will include a clear, balanced and detailed comparison of the hazards of alpha, beta and gamma radiation as a result of their different properties and the safe handling of radioactive material.

Examples of points made in the response:
- Nuclear radiation can kill cells:
  - causing sickness and/or death
  - (in lower doses) damaging DNA and leading to cancers or birth defects.
- Nuclear radiation is ionising/causes atoms to lose or gain electrons.
- Alpha, beta and gamma radiation have different hazards because of their different properties.
- Alpha is most ionising, least penetrating/travel shortest distance/a few cm through air.
- Alpha causes most harm when inside the body (i.e. close to cells).
- Beta is less ionising than alpha but more penetrating/travels a few metres through air.
- Beta is less harmful than alpha inside the body, may penetrate skin.
- Gamma is least ionising but most penetrating/travels many kilometres through air.
- Gamma is most harmful outside the body, but less harmful inside the body than alpha or beta.
- Precautions:
  - Keep samples in lead-lined containers – stops alpha, beta and most gamma from escaping.
  - Wear protective clothes (lead-lined perhaps) and goggles to prevent radiation reaching the skin.
  - Use tongs to handle samples – keeps the samples a greater distance away from the body, preventing alpha and beta radiation from reaching the user.
  - Use samples with relatively short half-lives so that they are quickly removed from the body/environment.
  - Radon gas is flushed from homes by fans to stop it building up.
  - Avoid flying or going down deep mines where background count is higher than normal.

This page has been left deliberately blank.

Published by Pearson Education Limited, Edinburgh Gate, Harlow, Essex, CM20 2JE.

www.pearsonschoolsandfecolleges.co.uk

Copies of official specifications for all AQA qualifications may be found on the AQA website: www.aqa.org.uk

Text and original illustrations © Pearson Education Limited 2013
Edited by Judith Head and Florence Production Ltd
Typeset and illustrated by Tech-Set Ltd, Gateshead
Cover illustration by Miriam Sturdee

The rights of Peter Ellis, Sue Kearsey and Nigel Saunders to be identified as authors of this work have been asserted by them in accordance with the Copyright, Designs and Patents Act 1988.

First published 2013

17 16 15 14 13
10 9 8 7 6 5 4 3 2 1

**British Library Cataloguing in Publication Data**
A catalogue record for this book is available from the British Library

ISBN 978 1 447 94217 7

**Copyright notice**
All rights reserved. No part of this publication may be reproduced in any form or by any means (including photocopying or storing it in any medium by electronic means and whether or not transiently or incidentally to some other use of this publication) without the written permission of the copyright owner, except in accordance with the provisions of the Copyright, Designs and Patents Act 1988 or under the terms of a licence issued by the Copyright Licensing Agency, Saffron House, 6–10 Kirby Street, London EC1N 8TS (www.cla.co.uk). Applications for the copyright owner's written permission should be addressed to the publisher.

Printed in Slovakia by Neografia

All images © Pearson Education

Every effort has been made to contact copyright holders of material reproduced in this book. Any omissions will be rectified in subsequent printings if notice is given to the publishers.

In the writing of this book, no AQA examiners authored sections relevant to examination papers for which they have responsibility.